PREACHING ON
SPECIAL OCCASIONS

VOLUME THREE

By the same author:
CHRISTIAN LIFE STYLE
ALL IN GOOD FAITH
OPEN THE DOORS
OPEN THE BOOK
I GIVE YOU THIS RING
MY LIVERPOOL LIFE
BECOMING AN ANGLICAN

PREACHING ON SPECIAL OCCASIONS

VOLUME THREE

Edward H. Patey

MOWBRAY

LONDON & OXFORD

F
23
100

Copyright © Edward H. Patey 1985

ISBN 0 264 67046 9

First published 1985
by A. R. Mowbray & Co. Ltd,
Saint Thomas House, Becket Street,
Oxford, OX1 1SJ

Typeset by Acorn Bookwork,
Salisbury, Wiltshire
Printed in Great Britain by
Spottiswoode Ballantyne Ltd, Colchester

British Library Cataloguing in Publication Data

Patey, Edward H.
  Preaching on special occasions.—(Mowbray's
  sermon outline series; v. 3)
  1. Church of England—Sermons   2. Sermons
  —Outlines, syllabi, etc.
  I. Title
  251'.02   BX5133

ISBN 0-264-67046-9

To my former colleagues on
The Principal Chapter of Liverpool Cathedral

Basil Naylor
Leslie Hopkins
Eric Corbett
Gordon Bates

whose sermons much enriched my understanding
of the faith and mission of the Church,
and who heard mine with brotherly charity
and forbearance.

CONTENTS

vii

ix

ACKNOWLEDGEMENTS

I wish to express my thanks to the following holders of copyright material printed in this book.

The Oxford and Cambridge University Presses for extracts from the New English Bible, © 1970.

Faber and Faber Ltd for ten lines of 'Burnt Norton' from *Four Quartets* by T. S. Eliot.

Messrs George Allen & Unwin (Publishers) Ltd for an extract from the *Autobiography of Bertrand Russell*.

Bishop Lesslie Newbigin for a quotation from *The Other Side of 1984* (World Council of Churches).

I am also grateful to: the organizations and institutions which invited me to preach to them on these special occasions;

Canon Cleverley Ford, the editor of this series, who helped me to prepare this material for publication;

Joyce Crabtree, my secretary in Liverpool, who typed many of these sermons with great accuracy, though not always in agreement with their content.

Edward H. Patey

INTRODUCTION

The preacher who takes his task seriously knows that every time he mounts the pulpit steps he must see it as a special occasion. Even if he is in a church where he preaches almost every Sunday of the year and knows by name every member of his congregation, it yet remains a special occasion. During the week he has studied and thought about the text he has chosen for his sermon, however familiar the passage may already be to him. The people to whom he will speak that Sunday, however intimately he knows them, bring with them into the church new hopes, fears, anxieties and joys. There is always the possibility that a stranger will be in church that morning, and what is spoken from the pulpit may prove to be either a word in season or a serious hindrance to his future spiritual growth. The preacher who dares to speak 'in the name of the Father and of the Son and of the Holy Spirit' should never prepare his material carelessly or present it casually. Every preaching occasion is privileged and special.

The sermons collected in this book were not, however, prepared for delivery in the normal course of regular Sunday preaching in a local parish church. Each one was spoken to a particular congregation gathered for a special occasion. They were addressed to a wide variety of people such as nurses, Rotarians, students, lawyers, sailors, bank employees, musicians and airmen. Congregations came together to celebrate specific occasions such as the Queen's Silver Jubilee, Shakespeare's birthday, United Nations Day, a school Founder's Day, Christian Aid Week, a village flower festival and much else.

These sermons are printed exactly as they were delivered. To have attempted to up-date or abbreviate them for publication would have obscured the particular character of 'special occasion' preaching, which must be firmly rooted in the immediate concerns which are in the minds of those present in the church at that moment. References will be found to such events (among others) as the Falkland Islands conflict, the assassination of John Lennon and a strike of social workers. Each sermon is thus anchored in the contemporary context in which it was given. This is in line with the teaching of the prophets of the Old Testament and of Jesus in the Gospels, where the proclamation emerges out of events of the day which would have been well known to those to whom the message was addressed. There is a brief introduction to each sermon which describes the occasion for which it was delivered, and gives the reason for the choice of text or subject.

Some of these addresses were obviously given on once-only occasions which are not likely to occur in the life of a local church. But, even so, the themes chosen for treatment on these occasions will find a place in the teaching programme of any church anywhere. Other occasions, such as the Queen's Accession, Christian Aid Week, the Week of Prayer for Christian Unity and United Nations Day can provide the preacher with regular opportunities for teaching important aspects of faith and life, year by year.

Those who have to prepare sermons for special occasions have to ask themselves certain essential questions. What sort of people will be in the congregation? What particular event or concern brings them to church? Where are the meeting points between their interests and the gospel of Jesus Christ? On many of these occasions, such as a Royal British Legion church parade, a service for senior citizens, a civic service or a flower festival, the congregation is likely to be composed of men and women of different denominations and none. The preacher must be sensitive to the likely mixture of the people who will be sitting in front of him as he goes into the pulpit. Many of them will be quite unfamiliar with 'churchy' language and biblical texts. That is why most of the sermons in this book make sparse use of religious language familiar to regular church attenders, and quotations from the Bible are also sparingly used. It is a mistake to think that a sermon is empty of theological or biblical content because it is not peppered generously with texts and ecclesiastical phrases. On the kinds of occasions illustrated in this book the business of the preacher is to proclaim the gospel in the language of everyday use.

If the occasion involves a special sphere of interest (Christian Aid, healing, the law, banking, music) or a particular organization (Rotary, Royal British Legion or a school) the preacher must do his homework in advance, taking the trouble to discover all the relevant information he can. If he does this, he will avoid giving the impression (which is sometimes given by ill-prepared sermons) that he is speaking either out of ignorance or lack of interest in the affairs which bring this particular group into the church.

The liturgical setting in which the address is placed is also important. All the sermons in this book were given within carefully prepared acts of worship. Preaching should never be seen in isolation from the devotional context in which it is placed. The message of the sermon, and the particular concern of those present, should find a clear focus in the acts of thanksgiving, penitence, intercession and dedication which precede and follow the sermon. Worship and preaching should always be conceived as a single whole. Those who attend services on special occasions should leave the church filled with the conviction that 'the people here are not only interested in God, they are interested in us too. And that makes us believe that God is also interested in us.' To achieve that response should certainly be the overall consideration of those who are called to preach on special occasions.

POWERLESS MAJESTY

on the Silver Jubilee of Queen Elizabeth II

Royal Occasions (such as the anniversary of the accession of the Sovereign to the throne) can provide the preacher with a valuable opportunity to meditate, within the perspective of the Christian Faith, on the nature of authority and the present state of the nation. This address was given in May 1977 at a service to celebrate the Silver Jubilee of Queen Elizabeth II attended by members of the Merseyside Magistrates Association. The character both of the occasion and the congregation suggested authority as an obvious theme. The Bible passages which provide the inspiration for the address are John 19.10–11 *and* Phil. 2.5–11.

1 *The Queen*

The evolution of the monarchy during the twenty-five years of the reign of Queen Elizabeth II, and, indeed, during the years before, when King George VI was on the throne, make a fascinating study in the on-going history of kingship in our nation. The monarch herself would now seem to be increasingly divested of power, increasingly censured at the slightest hint of political involvement (as in the row over her reference to devolution in her recent Westminster Hall speech before Parliament), increasingly subject to critical comment by satirists, cartoonists and Willie Hamilton, even greeted by slogans and demonstrations as in her Jubilee Australian tour. Yet the throne is certainly held in higher regard than ever by the great majority of British people, and remains the envy of those nations who have to put up with presidents.

The Queen seems to demonstrate a kind of powerless majesty—a strength apparently arising out of weakness. So that she, who in herself has no power over life and death, no power to change policy or guide national strategy, is yet much more a centre of unity and stability than the dictators and generalissimos who think they wield unlimited power, yet who only cause dismay, disunity and distrust, and are themselves in constant peril.

2 *Jesus Christ*

Do you remember that famous scene in another imperial palace? Here is Pilate, proud, aloof, Ambassador Plenipotentiary of the Roman Emperor. And standing before him, stripped and wounded, is a carpenter from Galilee?

'Do you know,' says Pilate, 'do you know that I have power to kill you and power to let you go free?' And the carpenter replies: 'You would have no power at all if it were not given you by God in trust.'

Pilate the all-powerful faces Jesus the powerless one. But it is Jesus who is the majesty. It is Jesus who reigns as king—not Pilate. (John 19.8–11)

3 *True authority*

Authority is a tricky game—not least for those who have greatness thrust upon them. Not only kings and rulers, popes and High Court judges, but lesser folk like magistrates and deans: the 'worships' and the 'very reverends' of this world. We quickly begin to discover that authority depends less and less on the handle other people choose to give us; more and more on what it is we are ourselves. Real authority does not come simply by putting on a crown, a wig, an epaulette, a mitre, a chain.

That great Roman Catholic theologian, Professor Hans Küng, once said this about authority. He was, I think, talking about popes and bishops, but he might have been talking about any of us who, in one way or another, care to think of ourselves as in authority. 'Authority,' he said, 'can no longer be allowed to rest on external title or office, but on inner authority. And this inner authority must be based on three things—personal quality, factual competence, and partnership.' In other words, authority rests on what you are like as a human being; on how competently you do your job; and on how well you work in partnership with others.

In the past some very odd characters have sat on royal thrones, episcopal chairs and seats of justice—odd characters shielded and protected by the outward trappings of office.

2

One of the many things that gives hope for the days in which we live is that it is less easy now to get away with bogus authority. In the end it is not the office that counts, but the man or the woman who holds the office. There is no substitute for personal integrity, and no cover up for the lack of it.

Conclusion

We count ourselves fortunate that this could not be better illustrated than in our royal family—in the Queen herself, in Prince Philip, in the Prince of Wales, and in the wonderful Queen Mother. Though even they, as all mortals must be, are only pale reflections of Jesus Christ—powerless majesty indeed—who became the humblest servant of all and in that servanthood showed what it is to be King of Kings and Lord of Lords.

2   FOR SUCH A TIME AS THIS

on the twenty-fifth anniversary of the Queen's accession

It is the task of the preacher to speak from time to time in the tradition of prophecy, and to help his hearers to discern the signs of the times. National occasions, such as the anniversary of the Queen's accession, can provide just such an opportunity. This address, given in Liverpool Cathedral, attempts to speak of those aspects of contemporary national life which are clearly contrary to the will of God, and to bear witness to the providence of God at work both within society and in the renewal of the Church. The title 'For such a time as this' comes from the sermon which William Temple preached at his enthronement as archbishop in Canterbury Cathedral in 1942. Behind Temple's words (quoted at the end of this address) can be sensed the authentic tradition of the Old Testament prophets who looked at the conditions of their national life, and dared to proclaim 'Thus Saith the Lord'.

1 *Taking stock*

We can rightly thank God today for the stability which Queen Elizabeth II has given to our nation's affairs, through the dignity and grace with which she has continued to fulfil her high and difficult office during the past quarter of a century. As we look at those who hold the highest places in other nations, we can, without unduly criticizing their systems, count ourselves fortunate in our institution of the monarchy, and fortunate, too, in the present incumbent of the throne.

Yet it is impossible to look back on the past twenty-five years without astonishment at the strange things which have befallen our nation during this time. Though the prospect of a short-lived oil bonanza from the North Sea promises that we shall soon be the envy of many a nation (for nations, like individuals quickly become jealous of one another), it remains a fact that in general our stock as a world power has fallen immeasurably. At home the post-war boom (felt more in the midlands than up here in the north) has given place to a recession which has not been equalled in severity since the reign of the Queen's grandfather. Well over a million are unemployed, and the likelihood is that the number will rise dramatically during the next few years. As a recently published study by the Department of the Environment has pointed out, areas of multiple deprivation in our great cities such as London, Birmingham and Liverpool remain a national scandal.

These mammoth problems are met by a nation deeply divided. Management and labour remain in an unhelpful state of confrontation. Left wing and right wing take up increasingly hardened positions at either extreme. Complex moral issues like nuclear disarmament, abortion and law enforcement are met by a simplistic polarization which throws the protagonists into widely opposing camps. And the great agony of Northern Ireland, in which the name of Christ is blasphemously invoked by either side in the cause of ideological conflict, is a constant reminder of what Jesus once said about a house divided against itself. (Mark 3.25–26)

We begin our Jubilee celebrations at a painful time in our history, and it is difficult to know whether the pain should be attributed to the agony of death throes, or of the travail which heralds a new birth.

2 *Signs of hope*

My faith is that we are witnessing a birth rather than a death. For there are many signs of hope: signs that people in many

4

different ways are striving genuinely to bring about a more just society. Despite the bad press the city of Liverpool gets from journalists coming north to spy out the land, there is another tale to be told. There are people who care very much about the mess our inner city has got into; who care that bridges of understanding and trust should be built between labour and management; who care that in this area around the cathedral one man in three is now out of work; who care about homeless young people, battered wives, racial discrimination, one-parent families, bad housing, vandalism and the lack of trust so many people have in their elected leaders. And there are a growing number of people who are prepared to express their caring in practical action by becoming community or social workers, or who choose to practise their profession or teach in schools in the down-town areas, or who give up hours of their time to voluntary service. Thank God that so many of our neighbours in this city long to bring unity, understanding and harmony to our polarized and segregated society.

3 *The Church in the midst*

In the middle of all this stands the Church of Jesus Christ. What of the health of the Church in England, this Jubilee year? Let me tell you that I am much more hopeful about the Church now than I was twenty-five years ago. And I dare to say this in spite of diminishing congregations, diminishing baptisms and confirmations, diminishing ordinations, diminishing influence and prestige in secular society, and despite what many people call a failure of nerve and even of faith. Despite all this, the signs are of birth in the Church, and not of death.

Nine years after the Queen's accession, the New Testament in the New English Bible was issued. Nine years later, the whole Bible was published. At the same time the Jerusalem Bible came out, and other new versions have followed or are in preparation. Has there ever been such activity in Bible scholarship, translation and publication as now?

Ten years after her accession the Queen was present at the consecration of Coventry Cathedral, and for years afterwards people came in their thousands from all over the world to see Basil Spence's marvellous building, and to be deeply moved

5

and challenged by it. Just before that time, Guildford Cathedral was completed. Shortly afterwards the Roman Catholic cathedrals in Liverpool and Clifton were consecrated. Recent years have seen in this country an upsurge of cathedral building and cathedral life unknown since the middle ages.

Eleven years after the Accession, Bishop John Robinson published his best-selling paperback *Honest to God*. When the dust of the controversy stirred by it had settled down, we saw that this was just a token of a much greater movement in theology in which windows have been opened to let the fresh winds of honest enquiry blow upon the stuffiness of the old dogmatism.

Think of the massive operation of world-wide compassion we call Christian Aid. It was only just coming into being when the Queen ascended to the throne. Or think of the liturgical winds of change which have mercifully blown through all our churches, soon to find expression in the publication of The Alternative Service Book 1980. At the heart of these changes has been the re-establishment of the Eucharist at the centre point of Christian worship, where it rightly belongs. There have lately also been encouraging signs that many church leaders are ready to declare that the gospel of Jesus Christ must involve the Christian in political, industrial and social affairs, prepared to risk being misunderstood, or of being accused of playing a political game, in order to proclaim the good news of the kingdom of God to the contemporary world.

Further grounds for hope are to be found in the great strides towards trust and unity amongst the separated churches. Who would have believed, twenty-five years ago, that here on Merseyside, with its long history of sectarian intolerance, the leaders of the Anglican, Roman Catholic, Methodist, Baptist and United Reformed Churches, together with the Salvation Army, would have agreed to raise the necessary funds jointly to appoint a Baptist minister to act on behalf of them all as the officer of their Ecumenical Council? Here in the churches of Merseyside the ball has been placed marvellously at our feet. If we cannot move forward together here, it cannot be done anywhere.

6

Conclusion

On St George's Day 1942, William Temple preached in Canterbury Cathedral at his enthronement as archbishop. He chose to speak of the new spirit of unity and mission which even then was coming into the world-wide Church, despite the divisions and horrors of war.

'As though in preparation for such a time as this,' he said, 'God has been building up a Christian fellowship which now extends into almost every nation and binds citizens of them all together in true unity and mutual love.'

This is precisely what I believe God is doing in our churches now, and it is 'in preparation for such a time as this'. Like all institutions, the Church often seems to be conservative, wanting to cling to the past and terrified of new challenges. But there are signs—marvellous signs—of God at work among us, challenging and fashioning an often reluctant Church, that it may become more truly his instrument to proclaim his gospel by word and action in his world, and at such a time as this.

3   THE MANY AND THE FEW

on Battle of Britain Sunday

Few services present the preacher with greater opportunities or more pitfalls than such occasions as Remembrance Sunday, Battle of Britain Day or Royal British Legion church parades. The theme is more or less dictated by the concern of the congregation to recall the achievements and comradeship of times of war, and to honour the memory of those who gave their lives in the service of their country. The pitfalls lie in the temptation to indulge in jingoism, nationalism or nostalgia, rather than to proclaim the gospel of Jesus Christ. The majority of those present at these services are too young to remember the events being commemorated, and may even suspect that the service is an attempt to glorify war. For this reason it is essential that the theme of the address should have a clear biblical and theological basis, illustrated not only by events from the past, but also from the contemporary scene. The address which follows was given on Battle of Britain Sunday 1972, which coincided with the close of the Munich Olympic Games which ended in violent tragedy. The 'Many and the Few' was the obvious theme for the address, but the scenes in Munich could not be ignored. The Bible passages upon which the address was built are Luke 6.28–36 *and* Rom. 8.37–39, *together with the picture of Jesus Christ on the cross, the One dying for the many.*

1 *The politics of violence*

The events in Munich last Wednesday were in tragic and staggering contrast to the opening jamboree ten days earlier in the fantastic Olympic stadium, when more than a thousand athletes from over a hundred countries marched into the arena in an impressive display of international co-operation. At the opening ceremony we caught a glimpse of one world, even if the unity there sprang from the comparative triviality of shared interest in hurdling or boxing or swimming or show jumping. But Wednesday brought us back to grim reality: naked, terrible violence burst out of the suspicion, hatred, greed and resentment of divided nations. There is no doubt that this is a violent world, and, I suppose, has always been so. But television has brought it right home into our sitting rooms with a compelling and hypnotic realism. If the first Sunday in Munich represented the human ideal, last Wednesday showed up the reality.

Down in Brighton the Trades Union Congress was also in action this week, though world events were stealing its accustomed thunder in the news media. But here, too, there were signs of violence though of a different nature, with the forcible expulsion of minority groups because they refused to toe the line with the big battalions.

And last week also in the building industry, pickets in Shrewsbury (some reportedly from Merseyside) appeared to have been using the same bully-boy tactics in imitation of the dockers on the north-east coast.

It looks as if more and more people have come to the conclusion that guns, fists, stones, abuse, and shouting down the other man so that he cannot get a hearing, are better ways of putting your own ideas across than the civilized face-to-face encounter of man with man as human beings.

Whatever views we may have about the Government's new Rent Act, the rowdyism and hooliganism reported from the council chambers of Liverpool and Birkenhead suggest that there are at least some citizens in our locality who want to return to jungle politics. Jungle politics are the politics of the bully. And a number of recent events in both political and industrial relationships give some evidence that bullying can be made to pay off.

2 *Taking Jesus seriously*

Turn from all this to the New Testament, and you will find that the teaching of Jesus is, quite frankly, embarrassingly at odds with the way that most of us are taught to think. Listen to this, for instance: *Love your enemies; do good to those who hate you; bless those who curse you; pray for those who treat you spitefully. When a man hits you on the cheek, offer him the other cheek too; when a man takes your coat, let him have your shirt as well. Treat others as you would like them to treat you. If you love only those who love you, what credit is that to you? ... You must love your enemies and do good, and you will have a rich reward. Be compassionate as your Father is compassionate.* (Luke 6.27–36).

3 *The promise of victory*

No wonder the modern world finds it hard to take Jesus seriously, if that is really the kind of thing he went about saying.

But suppose we did take it seriously, what then? Here the evidence of the way the first Christians looked at it is instructive. They were such a minority in a hostile world that they could not fight back or bully, even if they wanted to. Yet, as you read the New Testament, the note that comes through is one of overwhelming confidence as the lesson read to us just now showed magnificently: *We have been treated like sheep for slaughter—and yet, in spite of all, overwhelming victory is ours through him who loved us. For I am convinced that there is nothing in death or life, in the realm of spirits or superhuman powers, in the world as it is or in the world as it shall be, in the forces of the universe, in heights or*

9

depths—nothing in all creation can separate us from the love of God in Christ Jesus our Lord. (Rom. 8.37–39)

This suggests that real power may not be on the side of the battalions and the bullies after all.

The old story of David and Goliath has haunted the imagination of mankind for hundreds of years. And whenever a David in his weakness overcomes a bully many times his size, we get a hunch that there is some strange power at work in the universe, of greater strength than sheer brute force. The tremendous impact of the Battle of Britain lies in the mysterious and majestic victory of the few over the many. And in the heroic risk and sacrifice involved.

Certainly in the battle of good against evil, there is always risk to be taken and always sacrifice to be made. And the heart of Christianity is Jesus, who took the risk of having the whole world against him, and who was ready to sacrifice life itself in the cause of right.

4 *Searching for solutions*

It is hard to say how we should apply the plain teaching of Jesus today. To Vietnam, for instance, or Northern Ireland, or the great confrontations in industry. Though it is safe to say that if, somehow, Jesus could be taken seriously within these conflicts, it would be a very different story indeed.

And it is hard to tell how to apply the teaching of Jesus to modern-day questions of peace and war. Many Christians believe that pacifism and non-violence are the only answer. I think their numbers are growing, and I know they have the New Testament on their side. But other Christians, with equal sincerity, whilst recognizing the New Testament ideal, believe that, for the time being, practical common sense and prudence may dictate some controlled use of force for the preservation of peace.

And this may be true. Yet all the evidence shows that those who possess force in the end find it hard not to employ it for selfish ends. And force, when it is so employed, has the habit of leaving behind it at least as many new problems as the old ones it has solved. Perhaps power is such a dangerous thing to put into the hands of individual people or individual nations that sanity will only begin to come to the world when every nation has dared to risk sacrificing its sovereignty in favour of some world body.

Maybe there are no ready-to-hand solutions here. But that does not excuse every serious man and woman from thinking about these things seriously, and every Christian man and woman from thinking about them Christianly. In the meantime, in the more humble sphere in which we move day by day, we must keep an eye on the bullies and show them up for what they are worth, even if in showing them up we take the risk and make the sacrifice of siding with the few against the many—just as Jesus did.

4   THEY SHALL RISE AGAIN

celebrating the seventy-fifth anniversary of the Submariners Old Comrades Association

> *Members of the Old Comrades Association assembled for this act of celebration and commemoration from all over the country. Preliminary research had shown they would all be wearing the Association's badge bearing the words 'They shall rise again'. The motto also appears on the colours which would be presented at the altar during the service. This provided an obvious theme for the address, linking words which would be familiar to those present at the service with the central belief of the Christian faith.*

1 *Two mottoes*

I have been looking at your crest on the front of the service paper, and especially I have been looking at the two mottoes. Above are the words in English: 'They shall rise again'; below, the words in Latin, *Resurgam* which means 'I shall rise'.

I wonder precisely what these words are meant to mean. *They shall rise. I shall rise.*

Obviously they imply something more than the picture of a submarine sinking to the depths of the sea in order to rise again to the surface. Obviously more than that.

Indeed, I could only assume that you have actually dared to take words from the New Testament, words from the heart of the Gospel, and pin them to your badges, and so pin them to yourselves. 'They shall rise.' 'I shall rise.'

In which case, in this solemn service and in this great building I have a right to ask each and every one of you the searching question which the writing on your badge compels.

2 *Rising again*

What does it mean to you, this idea of resurrection—this idea of rising again?

In a short while we shall be having an act of remembrance. The naval padre will call us to remember those who have laid down their lives, and the trumpets will sound. Is this just an act of remembrance? Are you just recalling to mind old comrades known and unknown who are now dead and gone? The trumpets will sound not only the Last Post—the sound of good night and goodbye. They will also sound Reveille—the summons to wake up to a new morning and a fresh dawn. *They will rise.*

Is this just wishful thinking? I suppose if you have no religious faith it is. But our hymns and readings and prayers this afternoon—and this great cathedral itself dedicated to the risen Christ—tell quite another story. They tell of a faith in a living God who calls us to live with him in his eternity. And they tell of God's guarantee that this is so, in the life of a man called Jesus who was done cruelly to death, but of whom it was said only three days later: 'He is not here. He is risen.'

This was God's way of showing that the words on your badge are not a sham or a delusion or a cheat or a fraud. Through faith and trust in this same Jesus we share his resurrection life. Death is swallowed up in victory. In this faith the dead are not dead. They are living conquerors. I hope that when we come to the solemn remembrance in a moment you will silently reaffirm your faith in the risen Christ and in his power to call men and women to live with him in eternity. And if you haven't that faith, ask that you may find it—perhaps find it here today.

3 *Resurrection now*

This isn't just a matter of pie in the sky when you die. Christians are bold enough to declare that resurrection life is

12

something which can be lived already, here and now. If we've got faith in the possibility of the victory of love over hate, the victory of purity over lust, the victory of charity over greed, the victory of unselfishness over self-seeking, the victory of humility over pride, the victory of life over death, we can rise above all that wants to submerge us, wants to drag us down, wants to smother us. We can live risen lives already.

Perhaps also, in the solemnity of the remembrance soon to follow, you can think not only of others but also of yourself: of what may be dragging you down and preventing your resurrection now. I mean things like problems at home, at work, money, neighbours, employment, family, friends; or problems right inside yourself—fear of illness, fear of the future, fear of death, fear of sin, fear of guilt. I know that so many people make a misery of their own lives and of the lives of other people, because they are not able to rise above the things that drag them down. They continue to live submerged lives.

Our Christian faith does not underestimate the power of evil in the affairs of the world nor in the hearts of men and women. The Bible is full of graphic accounts of it. Often it uses the very picture of a drowning man sucked down into the sea's lowest depths. But our Christian faith holds out the promise of rescue. A power comes from prayer and faith and love and honest self-knowledge and humility and penitence. It is the power which lets us rise above the things which get us down. Our Christian faith promises here and now the possibility of a resurrection life—a rising above all that imprisons and suffocates. This is the hall-mark of the man of faith. In the silent moment of remembrance in which we shall soon all share, ask for the strengthening of your faith if you already have it. And ask for the finding of faith if you have lost it or never had it.

4 *Present and future*

And one last thing. If you are able to take quite seriously what I have been trying to say, you will find that you will no longer be content with the future tense in your motto. You will want to bring it right into the present. Of the dead whom we will soon remember, you will want to say not 'They shall rise again', but that in Christ they are already victorious, risen, and alive. It is not the dead we shall be commemorating in the solemn silence, but those who are far more alive than any of us here today.

And as for *Resurgam*, 'I shall rise'. That is my hope, and I hope it is yours, for we are already rising now, already sharing in Christ's resurrection now, because we are getting the better already of the things that want to drag us down.

5   ATLANTIC CONFLICT

commemorating victory in the Battle of the Atlantic

This was a difficult sermon to prepare. The occasion was the annual commemoration of victory in the Battle of the Atlantic (the Western Approaches) in the Second World War, to which past and present members of the Royal Navy come to Liverpool Cathedral in large numbers. The problem was that when the time for this service came in 1982, another battle in the Atlantic was on everybody's mind as the Naval Task Force was arriving in the Falkland Islands zone. Already the more popular newspapers were indulging in extremes of jingoism which were clearly at odds with the Christian faith. It seemed, therefore, necessary to use this occasion to place the emphasis on the personal responsibility of each individual in that part of life where he can have some influence. The Bible texts which underlie this address are Matt. 15.19 *and* Matt. 25.21.

1 *Two Easter services*

As we meet today to remember the events which took place in the North Atlantic forty years ago, our thoughts are inevitably focused on the events now taking place in the South Atlantic around the Falkland Islands.

I could avoid that subject altogether, probably to the relief of everyone. Yet in a building dedicated to the gospel of Christ and to the harnessing of that gospel in the down-to-earth quest for the realization of the kingdom of God, it would be to shirk the spiritual challenge of the moment not to ask what religious truths, if any, can be learned from the nerve-wracking events of the past four weeks.

14

I find myself haunted by the pictures which appeared on our television screens of two Easter services: one on board one of Her Majesty's ships of the Task Force, when young men crowded in for worship led by their naval padre; the other, when we saw hundreds of Argentinians, many of them also young, pouring out of the cathedral into the streets of Buenos Aires after their Easter mass. What would have been in the minds of those two lots of Christians each celebrating the resurrection victory of Jesus Christ? Here is a fact of history, often repeated, with Christian apparently praying against Christian. It is, I suppose, the prospect of such a contradiction which might give Pope John Paul second thoughts about his visit to this country, and indeed to this cathedral, later this month.

2 *National pride*

The Christian faith is, for all our human divisiveness, a great, world-wide, international family. Jesus called his followers his brothers and sisters, and this, according to the New Testament, puts believing Christians of every nation into a closer relationship with one another than that of blood or nationality. This international perspective is one of the clearest teachings of Holy Scripture, though time and time again in history it has been obscured by national pride and racial prejudice. Nationalism is the enemy of Christianity, and national pride no less than personal pride may contain the seeds of its own destruction, as the Bible clearly teaches.

The Bishop of Durham wrote in a telling letter in *The Times* newspaper last Friday: 'A subtle process begins when putting the "Great" back into Great Britain becomes an unacknowledged war aim'.

Yet it is not as easy as that. When it comes down to concrete situations, as it has over the past four weeks, everything becomes bewilderingly complex in a blinding mix of conflicting emotions: the incredible skill of the men and women of our forces, combining personal daring, technical know-how, devotion to duty, loyalty and discipline; the tragic plight of those sheep-farming islanders whose peaceful and pastoral way of life has been so roughly disturbed by illegal invasion; the constant political manoeuvring of the great powers for advantage in the balance of might in the southern hemisphere; the hopes and fears about the yet-to-be-exploited mineral wealth of Antarctica; the sinister implications of the international arms trade, and the threat to its purveyors that, like Hamlet's engineer, they might be hoist with their own petard.

No wonder we find ourselves caught up in a situation where it is hard to see absolutely clearly what the right course of action should be. Yet, because (in R. A. Butler's famous phrase) politics is the art of the possible, governments have to decide one way or another on actions, and executives have to carry them out as best they know how. This is why one Christian thing that can clearly be said at this moment is that our Prime Minister and Foreign Secretary and the diplomats and service chiefs who have to carry out their policies, need our prayers and should have them.

3 *No easy solution*

Can our religious faith really help here? In one sense the answer is No. Neither our prayers nor our Bible study nor our worship will bring quick solutions falling down from heaven. The religion of Jesus and the Bible is not a kind of magic. It does not offer instant remedies. Indeed, in one sense it may actually make things more difficult because it insists that, in every moral problem, whether it is the break-up of a marriage, a dispute between management and labour in industry, racial tension in our streets, or conflict between nations, self-interest and expediency can never be the sole or ultimate criterion.

For the Christian the absolute priority is love—that is to say a deep-down concern for the well-being of others. This is the overriding requirement of the Christian ethic. Such love is based not on the ten commandments nor on any code of laws, but on the total self-giving of Christ on the cross. For the Christian the cross is the one, true, authentic symbol of the quality of love, the cost of love and the extent to which love must go.

This is an ethic which is difficult enough to work out in our own small, personal situations. When it comes to the great social, economic, and political facts of life, it becomes more difficult still. That is why we must not be surprised to find Christians of equal intelligence, integrity, compassion and

16

holiness coming down on opposite sides in, for example, the pacifist or nuclear disarmament debate. And the awkward thing is that both sides may be right in so far as each is sticking out for an important aspect of the truth, and both may be wrong because the necessary practical solution may always be an oversimplification of a complex moral issue.

Yet, hard though it may be, as Christians we cannot opt out of the struggle involved in trying to relate the teaching of Jesus to the great perplexities of the modern world. To see religion as only relevant to personal piety is to be only half-converted. Discipleship demands the courage to face the tough issues of life in the light of our faith even though answers can only begin to emerge slowly, painfully and always partially. Inevitably, even the wisest and the holiest of us will, in St Paul's words, see as through a glass darkly.

Yet there is a more immediate response we can make. The conflicts and anxieties of the international scene are only versions greatly magnified, of the things we know go on deep down inside each one of us. *From out of the heart*, said Jesus, *proceed evil thoughts, murder, adulteries, fornications, thefts, false witness, blasphemies.* (Matt. 15.19–20)

4 *Personal responsibility*

Are not the things which fill the newspapers—South America, Northern Ireland, the Middle East, Poland, Afghanistan—are not these, in essence, precisely the same things, though vastly magnified, as those which determine so much of our own private thoughts and actions?

We say a country has broken international law, but what about the motorist who persistently drives through the light signals when they have turned from yellow to red, or who ignores the speed restrictions on a motorway in a fog and risks the lives of others, assuming that although the law may apply to other people, he somehow is exempt or can get away with it? We say a country ignores its treaty obligations, yet how many political promises and commercial agreements are ratted on, and how many marriages in no time lay aside the solemn promises made on the wedding day?

We blame a country for grabbing what does not belong to it, yet how many millions of pounds are lost annually to the

17

exchequer by tax fiddling, and to our transport authorities by fare dodging? We are rightly critical of the racial policies of South Africa, but no one can be proud of racial attitudes in our own land, particularly in the matter of equal job opportunities for black and white. We talk of the callousness of dictator states, yet hospital workers seem ready to turn their backs on the sick, and cemetery workers to add further sorrow to the bereaved by taking strike action for their own—no doubt legitimate—claims. Though we rightly condemn oppression in regimes both of the right and left, many people in our communities suffer stress from the exercise of power by petty bureaucrats in their dealings with their customers or their clients.

To say this is not to solve the great crises of our times. But it is to put them into some kind of perspective, and to remind us that global problems have their origins in the hearts of individual men and women. You and I may not be able to solve the Falkland crisis or the running sore of Northern Ireland. But we can do something about the same kinds of factors which worry and hassle us in those small local spheres of influence in which we live our lives. If a start is to be made anywhere in trying to take seriously Christ's kind of loving, with all the care, concern, discipline and sacrifice it must involve ... then this is the place to start, where we can have some influence, where we can make some impact. For the problems which beset mankind are all of a piece.

By making that kind of start, where we are now, we may begin to see the part we may play in the broader picture as we hear the Lord's words of encouragement and approval. *Well done, good and faithful servant. You have proved trustworthy in a small way. I will put you in charge of something big.* (Matt. 25.21)

6   CONQUEST OF THE SEAS

at a Trafalgar Day Service

The first English prayer book was being composed in the lifetimes of Francis Drake and Walter Raleigh, when England was becoming one of the world's major sea powers.

18

Since those days there has always been a close connection between the English Church and those who 'go down to the sea in ships'. Today many churches in seaside towns have annual services for seafarers. Two examples are given here. At the first, held annually in honour of Horatio Nelson in Portsmouth, the lesson was read by Alec Rose, a local man, who had recently completed a successful solo round-the-world voyage in a small sailing craft.

1 Down to the sea in ships

It was the Polish seaman who became one of the greatest masters of the English language, Joseph Conrad, who once said that England was the country where men and the sea interpenetrate. Certainly no one in this island lives very far from the sea, and I suppose salt water courses through our veins as it does through the veins of Norwegians, Dutch and Portuguese. This is why the sea—often the cruel sea—plays such a role in English literature: Shakespeare's *Tempest*, Coleridge's *Ancient Mariner*, Kipling's *Captains Courageous*. And this is why, even in an age of scientific miracles and space exploration, the exploits of Thor Heyerdal crossing the Southern Seas on Kontiki, and Francis Chichester and Alec Rose circumnavigating the globe single-handed, stir the heart and the imagination as few things can.

For the same reason, I suppose, thousands of men and women forsake their offices and shops and factories at weekends to mess about in boats, and to become sailors for a few hours in their yachts and dinghies and power craft.

But the sea is not primarily a place for poets, holiday-makers or adventurers—though it serves them all well. It is, as you well know here in Portsmouth, part of that very arterial system by which the industry and commerce of the nation is kept moving. It is the vital highway by which peoples communicate with one another on the world's business. And on this highway the merchantmen are the commercial travellers, the navies are the police patrols, and the life-boats and coast-guards the ambulance and rescue services. Block those highways, and we are in peril.

The opening up of these sea lanes is an epic story. The men who set out from our ports in centuries gone by, bound for unknown destinations, in frail craft, with no power but the wind, and no guide but the stars—these are among the great heroes of our island's history. As is, in a unique way, Horatio Nelson, whose memory we especially honour today who, over a century and a half ago, maintained the right of seafarers to go about on their lawful occasions on the high seas.

2 *The sea highways*

Radar, modern navigational aids, and propeller power, have revolutionized sea communications. But today's safety and certainty as ships go about their business owes an incalculable debt to generations of intrepid seafarers who opened up the way—often at the cost of terrible hardship, and sometimes of life itself.

And even today, with all that modern science and technology can do, rocks and currents may still be hazards, and wind and weather play cruel tricks on the sturdiest vessel. For this great highway the sea can still be a barrier and a snare; as it was all that time ago when the Egyptian Pharaoh perished in the Red Sea whilst in hot pursuit of the runaway Israelites, or when St Paul was shipwrecked in the Mediterranean.

But on the whole, the ancient Jews, unlike their near neighbours the Phoenicians, were not particularly interested in the sea. As often as not in the Old Testament the sea is spoken of in fear, whilst in the New Testament the seas in which the sailor-fishermen disciples of Jesus earned their living, were inland lakes with their own particular treachery.

3 *Breaking down barriers*

To most biblical writers, the sea was a barrier which had to be negotiated before the safety of the harbour could be reached. And you may remember how St John, of the last book of the Bible, banished for his faith by the Roman authorities to a lonely island in the middle of the Mediterranean, had a vision of the time when the sea would be no more, with all barriers down and no more separation. (Rev. 21.1)

And I remember once having a conversation at a meeting on European Unity with that redoubtable and royal lady Queen Wilhelmina of Holland, and saying something about the Channel being a barrier between England and the continent—and her quick and incisive reply: 'If you are a Christian—there is no Channel.'

The sea is there to be conquered, and distance to be annihilated so that the barriers between nation and nation can be done away with, and the peoples of the world have total access, one with another. And this will require even greater sacrifice than has been necessary for the opening up of the sea lanes, and the protection and rescue of the ships which do it. For the barriers of the mind which create narrow nationalism, and the prejudices and pride which make one nation exploit another nation; which make one race despise another race; which make people want to lord it over other people; which make the rich want to go on being rich at the expense of the poor, and the strong go on being strong at the expense of the weak—these are barriers which are more dangerous, more treacherous, and more difficult to overcome than any ocean. We need a new Nelson to do battle on the cruel seas of national and international affairs. Yes, and we need a breadth of vision to take a world view, to be able to stand on other people's shores and see ourselves through their eyes rather than our own, that is in a less familiar, less flattering but probably truer light, from their vantage point.

We need, too, a faith to chart a way through the tricky seas of wrongful ambition in the name of the God who was lifted high above the dividing oceans of the world, lifted on a cross in order to draw all men to himself—and to one another. All men. On each side of every sea. Everywhere.

7   GOD SAW THAT IT WAS GOOD

at a service for seafarers

The second example of a sermon concerned with the sea was given at the annual seafarers' service in the parish church of St Andrew in Plymouth. Plymouth is a famous and ancient seaport, an important naval base, and a popular holiday resort. The congregation consisted of naval personnel, seafarers (professional and amateur), civic representatives, and members of the general public. The obvious theme was God as

21

*Creator, and man's use (or misuse) of the seas and coastline.
The text, with which the sermon began was* God said Let the
waters under heaven be gathered into one place so
that dry land may appear; and so it was. God called
the dry land earth and the gathering of the waters he
called seas, and God saw that it was good. (Gen.
1.9–10).

1 *The good Creator*

The unknown poetical genius who wrote the first chapter of
Genesis saw the division of the earth's surface into oceans and
dry land as part and parcel of God's good creative purpose.
And those of us who live beside the sea, or whose livelihood is
to do with the sea, must surely believe this to be true.

God saw that it was good. A sentimental poet once declared
that you are nearer to God in a garden than anywhere else on
earth. I don't believe it. I believe you are nearer to God
through people, and often through unlikely people in unlikely
places. But if I'm looking for God in nature, I think I find him
most where ocean and dry land meet, for instance, between
Bolt Head and Bolt Tail where I walked along the South
Devon coast path on Friday. As a Devonian, now working in
the highly industrial north, I found wonderful refreshment in
the incomparable coastline of my native county.

The book of Genesis is right to begin the whole Bible story
with a celebration of God's goodness in creation, just as the
creeds begin with the confident assertion 'I believe in God, the
Father Almighty, maker of heaven and earth'. For the good of
our spirits, we all need to enjoy the created world, the sight
and sound and feel of the sea and sky and earth, just as our
bodies need vitamins and proteins for their proper health. To
be under-exposed to the miracle and mystery of God's world is
to be spiritually starved. There is a religious dimension to the
trip to the seaside and to the moors, mountains, canals, lanes
and villages of our land. If these things open up visions of the
handiwork of our Creator God, holidays can indeed become
holy days.

The simple theological truth that God is Creator raises a
number of immediately practical issues. It means that every
man, woman and child has the right as well as the need of
access to the places of greatest beauty—to the coasts and to

the hills. It means that every man, woman and child has a right to the time and means to enjoy the good things of the created world which God has given us to share. And it means that God is blasphemed in our great cities such as Liverpool or Glasgow because children grow up in slums, starved of natural beauty and, in consequence, tragically unable to recognize natural beauty when at last they have the opportunity of seeing it.

2 *Exploitation*

It also means that there is a solemn moral duty laid upon us to ensure that man's greed and carelessness are not allowed to despoil the beauty that God has provided. It is now fashionable to jump on the environmental and ecological bandwagon, but we have started to talk about it when it is almost too late. If only we had had a more lively sense of God as Creator we would have sounded the alarm long ago. We would just not have tolerated much of that hideous ribbon development which has messed up our coastline. We would not have tolerated the gallons of untreated sewage poured into the sea from our seaside boroughs and industrial installations. We would not have allowed the circumstances which permit such environmental tragedies as those massive oil spills from tankers like that off the East Anglian coast this week. It isn't just that this threatens the holiday industry on the Norfolk Broads. The survival of God-created natural life is itself at stake. Too often man destroys what God has created.

The seas and the coasts are not only places of recreation and refreshment—they are also places of work, part of the industrial scene and vital to our economic survival. First, and from time immemorial, the catching and marketing of fish. Now, more recently, the seas have other gifts to bring, the source of vital supplies of gas and oil. And in the future, as man exhausts the potential of the dry land, the untold wealth of the sea bed offers new opportunities for exploration and exploitation.

But if man has not yet learned how to share fairly and equitably the products of the land, is he likely to fare any better with the as yet untapped resources of the oceans themselves?

Throughout history men have scrambled for land, scrambled

for power, scrambled for gold, for oil, for gas, scrambled to be first to put their national flags on a desert island, on a dead moon, on an uninhabited planet. I dread to think how in future years the ocean bed may become the new arena for greed, with what terrible wastage of energy, of resources, of imagination, of skill, of human life.

Perhaps more than on anything else, the future of mankind depends on a restatement of the fundamental Christian ethics of reconciliation, peace, unselfishness, brotherhood and sacrifice in our dealings with one another. This is especially important in our future dealings with the oceans of our planet.

3 *Stewardship*

Is the world ours to play about with? Do we really think that we own the earth or the sea or the sky? We do not. 'The earth is the Lord's,' says the Bible. And so is the sea. We are merely temporary trustees. The sea was here long before man emerged on the scene. The sea will still be here millions of years after the last vestiges of human existence have left this planet. The drama of creation will reach its climax unnoticed by human eyes, or experienced by human brains. The sea will outlast all of us. The sea, like the mountains, puts us in our place. I once interviewed John Hunt, shortly after he had led his team to the summit of Everest. I asked the typical journalist's question: 'What makes you want to climb a mountain?' He didn't give the stock answer: 'Because it is there'. He said something more. 'Because,' he said, 'it humbles you. For the mountain range is so huge and man so insignificantly small.'

I was looking again the other day at Sir Francis Chichester's account of his solo voyage round the world. Rounding Cape Horn in those mountainous seas ... the tiny 'Gipsy Moth' and one middle-aged man in it.

The prophet Isaiah described it wonderfully in his account of the creative work of God.

> *Who has gauged the waters in the palm of his hand,*
> *Or with its span set limits to the heavens?*
> *Who has held all the soil of earth in a bushel,*
> *Or weighed the mountains on a balance,*
> *Or the hills on a pair of scales,*
> *Who has set limits to the spirit of the Lord?* (Isa. 40.12–13)

Here is the paradox. It is when man learns that kind of humility that he discovers his full stature. The more science and technology put power into our hands, the more it is absolutely crucial that we learn what it is to be humble: to know our small place in Creation. Power without humility is death. It is from power placed at the service of humility that there comes the possibility of resurrection.

So it is that if you seek a sign to symbolize man's rightful control over the created world which he holds in a very temporary stewardship, it is neither the mushroom cloud of Hiroshima nor the clenched fist of the revolutionary—it is a crucified figure on a green hill outside a city wall, with arms outstretched to all humanity in love that is totally humble and self-giving.

8   OUR CHRISTIAN HERITAGE

celebrating Christian Heritage Year

The announcement that 1984–85 would be designated as Christian Heritage Year was not received with much enthusiasm by many church leaders. Nevertheless it was observed in many places and many special sermons must have been preached to suit the occasion. This address was given at an ecumenical and civic service in a Dorset church on the Sunday in 1984 which also marked the beginning of Christian Aid Week. The service began with a pageant by Sunday School pupils illustrating the Christian heritage of the neighbourhood. It concluded with prayers for Christian Aid Week, and the commissioning of collectors. These themes had to be amalgamated in the address.

1 *Building Jerusalem*

We began this service with that much loved hymn of William Blake, *Jerusalem*. Blake wrote, you may remember, at the height of the Industrial Revolution when men, women and children worked long hours, under appalling conditions, in dark, noisy factories, for abysmally low wages. If you had talked to them about the English Christian Heritage, they would probably not have known what you meant. If you went on to tell them that you were talking about William Shake-speare, John Bunyan, Thomas Cranmer, Henry Purcell, John Milton, George Herbert, Wells Cathedral and the Lindisfarne Gospels, they would not have understood either. In the early nineteenth century these things were for the upper crust of society: the working classes only had leisure to get enough rest for the next week of over-work.

Perhaps that is why Christian Heritage Year has been received with some cynicism, not least amongst the churches themselves, where it has been described as ecclesiastical jingoism, giving a halo to British tourism. The Archbishop of Canterbury himself voiced some of these criticisms in the inaugural service in Westminster Abbey last Wednesday, when he said that we must not allow this observance to encourage that sense of superiority of which the British have sometimes been guilty, or blind us to the crisis now upon our country and the needs of the many people who felt themselves (as he put it) excluded from the banquet of affluence. It is only too easy to romanticize about the past in order to bolster up our sense of national well-being for the present.

William Blake was a romantic, too, but he was also a realist. As he wrote his famous hymn he focused his attention (as he does ours) on the dark satanic mills, the only heritage which the industrial workers of his day knew about. That is why he looked to the future when injustice and squalor would be removed from our national life, and Jerusalem would be built in England's green and pleasant land.

What followed in England immediately after Blake was the age of Queen Victoria, an age which, in so many ways, added vastly to our Christian heritage. It was one of the great periods of church building, of the founding of many of our finest schools, of the Oxford Movement which brought colour and dignity back to the rather tired, dull Anglican Church of the time. It marked the beginning of many of our great social work organizations such as Dr Barnardo's, the Children's Society, the Salvation Army, the Boys' Brigade, the YMCA and YWCA. A host of great names are there such as Thomas Arnold, Charles Dickens, William Ewart Gladstone, John Keble, Elizabeth Fry, Charles Kingsley, Florence Nightingale, David Livingstone, Cardinal Newman, Josephine Butler, Lord Shaftesbury, Charles Villiers Stanford. It was an age of

26

remarkable achievement, and an age of great hope with its eyes firmly on the future. People were able to go to church and sing with confidence:

Nearer and nearer draws the time,
the time that shall surely be,
When the earth shall be filled with the glory of God
as the waters cover the sea.

2 *The failure of a vision*

What has happened to us since? Vast advances in scientific research have brought us to the brink of nuclear holocaust, while tying up in armaments a vast proportion of the world's wealth, so badly needed for more constructive purposes. Great strides in medical and surgical techniques have, thank God, got rid of many of the former killer diseases (in the rich countries, anyway), but they have given place to subtler and equally dangerous diseases to do with the disorientation and disillusionment of the human person. Having long proclaimed that man has a right to work because he is made in the image of God the worker, we now see millions of our fellow men and women thrown on the scrap heap of unemployment and redundancy. Despite the sophistication of the new science of personnel management, human relations seem to be reaching a low ebb with various groups in our society unable or unwilling to talk to one another, or to listen to one another. As Disraeli said, a century ago, they seem to belong to two separate nations. With all those pop songs about love and all those books about sex, you would have thought that we might have reached some maturity in our understanding of the relationship between men and women. Instead, we have the astronomical failure of nearly half those who get married today to make a success of it. And most serious of all for the future of mankind, more serious even than the nuclear threat, is that ever-widening gap between rich and poor, with the wealthy nations (the minority) getting richer, and forever trying to raise their standards of living even higher, whilst the poorer nations (the majority) get poorer all the time.

Do you begin to wonder what we have done with the Christian heritage we are supposed to be celebrating this year?

Bishop Lesslie Newbigin has analysed these problems in a

recently published essay which he calls *The Other Side of 1984*. He writes of the dramatic suddenness with which, in the space of one lifetime, our civilization has lost confidence in its own validity. 'The loss of confidence in the future is expressed eloquently in the mindless folly of the petty vandalism of those who can only express their rage by smashing up the symbols of meaningless affluence, and the equally mindless madness of the nuclear arms race between the super powers. The mushroom clouds which rose into the sky above the blasted ruins of Hiroshima and Nagasaki have, ever since that day in 1945, hung in menace over the consciousness of modern men and women, posing with fearful poignancy the question "Is there a future for civilization as we know it?"'

3 *Who builds Jerusalem?*

At the start of the service we sang with William Blake:

> *I will not cease from mental fight,*
> *Nor shall my sword sleep in my hand*
> *Till we have built Jerusalem*
> *In England's green and pleasant land.*

You may think that we have not made much progress in that building operation since those words were written a century and a half ago. And this may be because we persist in making the mistake which Blake himself seems to have made, in thinking that it is *we* who can build Jerusalem in England's green and pleasant land. That was the characteristic optimism of the Victorians which has been so rudely shattered in our time. The poet W. E. Henley, born just twenty years after Blake's death, was able to express the mood of his times with absolute confidence.

> *I am the master of my fate,*
> *I am the captain of my soul.*

You only have to look at the headlines in your newspapers or on television to know that this is a lie. Men have tried to build their Jerusalem relying solely on their own ideas, on political theory, or the scientific method, or on economic panaceas such as Marxism or monetarism. But there is no sign of the new Jerusalem.

If you want to know why that is so, turn to your Bible and to another visionary poet who wrote in the book called

28

Revelation: 'I saw the holy city, new Jerusalem, coming down out of heaven from God.' (Rev. 21.2)

From God. It is not we who build the city. The letter to the Hebrews talks about a city with firm foundations, 'whose architect and builder is God'. (Heb. 11.10) It is God who offers us the plans of the city for our acceptance, and who provides the blueprint which is what Jesus called the kingdom of God. And the secret of that kingdom is love, compassion, humility and self-sacrifice. Its badge is a cross. And its law is a new commandment, 'Love one another'. Our urgent need is not to preserve a Christian heritage from the past, but to grasp, as if it were a new thing, the essential claim of Christ upon ourselves our nation and our world.

Few things exhibit Christ's kind of loving more powerfully than what 400,000 volunteers up and down the country are poised to do this week distributing Christian Aid envelopes ready for action on behalf of those who live their lives in the world's most hopeless situations. Action in the name of Christ to help the poor, the oppressed, the discriminated against, the persecuted in this unequal and unjust world.

Making it clear for all to see that the Christian heritage, which we in our comfortable churches want to pass on, must be our conviction that there will be no Jerusalem in England's green and pleasant land, or anywhere else for that matter, until we all come to recognize that our own standard of living, either as a nation or as an individual, is nothing like so important for the future of mankind as our standard of loving.

9   BUILDING COMMUNITY

at a Royal British Legion Church Parade

It is the custom for members of the Royal British Legion and their friends to attend an annual parade of remembrance and dedication in the parish church which serves their district. Many of the men and women who come to these services will not be regular churchgoers, and their attendance will owe more to their allegiance to the Legion than to their religious faith. If the preacher is to use this opportunity to gain a hearing for the gospel, he must first show some knowledge of the aims of the British Legion, and sympathy for its work. If he is able to do this, his message may be heard with appreciation.

When, in 1971, the Royal British Legion celebrated its Jubilee, a fascinating book appeared to mark the occasion. Under the title *Red for Remembrance*, the author gave a graphic account of the first fifty years of the Legion's history, and looked with confidence to its future.

Picking up the book again after a number of years I found particularly poignant the Foreword written by the Admiral of the Fleet, Earl Mountbatten, who had done so much to help the victims of war through his Presidency of the British Commonwealth Ex-Service League, and who was himself to die soon after, blown to pieces in his yacht by IRA terrorists. I was particularly struck by this sentence in Lord Mountbatten's preface: 'In the Legion,' he said, 'we have dedicated ourselves to the principles of maintaining democracy and peace.'

1 *Democracy*

What do you think that word democracy means? Do we talk about it too easily and understand it too little? There is an old Latin tag, *Vox populi, vox dei*: 'the voice of the people is the voice of God'.

Some folk like to believe that, but it is clearly nonsense. The majority are quite often wrong. The records which top the charts in the hit parade are not the best pieces of music available, any more than the Eurovision Song Contest picks out the best song, or Miss World picks out the most beautiful woman. The majority vote in Parliament, or on the city council, or at a Party Conference, or a Trades Union Congress often turns out to be the wrong decision. Time and time again, it is those in the minority who are proved to be right. Remember Jesus on the cross when all forsook him and fled. Jesus was in a minority of one.

As W. R. Inge, the great Dean of St Paul's once said: 'Democracy is an experiment in Government which has the disadvantage of counting votes instead of weighing them.'

So we must not fall into the trap of believing, as some do,

that democracy is a kind of alternative religion, or is even necessarily the best form of government we can devise. I doubt whether Lord Mountbatten, who was every inch an aristocrat, believed in that kind of thing.

What I guess he was after when he said that the task of the Royal British Legion was to maintain democracy, was something a good deal deeper, a good deal more difficult, and a good deal more Christian.

2 *A deeper meaning*

Let me explain what I mean, and under three headings. When I talk about democracy, I think I mean the organization of our life together in the community in such a way that:

(a) each holds his fellow human beings in respect,
(b) each believes in the rule of law,
(c) each knows that service to others ought to have priority over service to oneself.

These three things: mutual respect, law and service, all find support in the Bible.

(a) *Mutual respect.* Our life together in the community is destroyed when we categorize, stereotype, or denigrate those who happen to belong to a different race, political party, social class, or religious persuasion from ourselves. To do this is to be like the mindless people who throw eggs at politicians, organize marches to stir up racial hatred, or roughly shout down those they do not agree with, like the people who shouted down the Archbishop of Canterbury in Liverpool Parish Church earlier this year. These are the enemies of true democracy. That is why the self-confessed agnostic Voltaire was nearer the truth than some so-called Christians when he declared 'I disapprove of what you say, but I defend to the death your right to say it'. More positively St Paul, writing to the Ephesians said: 'Have done with spite and passion, all angry shouting and cursing and bad feeling of every kind. Be generous to one another, tender-hearted and forgiving.' (Eph. 4.32)

Can the Legion, with its thousands of members, help lead our nation away from intolerance and confrontation to a sensible and sensitive mutual respect for one another as human beings?

(b) *Law.* An essential ingredient of true democracy is respect

31

for the rule of law. The opposite of democracy is anarchy, and I was disturbed to hear a Member of Parliament on the BBC this week, on the subject of secondary picketing and so-called sympathy strikes, advocating the breaking of laws you don't happen to agree with. All governments pass bad laws as well as good ones, and the job of everyone in a democracy is to use all lawful means to get bad laws changed. But civil disobedience can only be justified morally in quite exceptional cases, as, for instance, under an oppressive dictatorship—and may it never apply to us in Britain. Acts of Parliament cannot in themselves make people virtuous, but laws, by and large, do serve to protect the weak from the bully boys. Deliberate law breaking such as I heard advocated by that MP and by some trade union leaders, always weakens the fabric of society.

Let us go to St Paul again, and remember what he said to his fellow Christians in Rome: 'Every person must submit to the supreme authorities. There is no authority but by act of God, and the existing authorities are instituted by him.' (Rom. 13.1–3) And remember that Paul wrote those words when the civil authority was none other than the cruel Emperor Nero, and hundreds of Christian men and women were suffering martyrdom at his hands.

Can the Legion, with its thousands of members, help the nation to return to a respect for law, and to a wider sense of responsibility to see that those who get into positions of power, make wise laws and ensure that those laws are administered fairly?

(c) *Service*. I have mentioned respect for one another and respect for the law. Now I come to the spirit of service. Need I say much about this to a congregation of British Legion members whose organization is dedicated to service? Perhaps not. Yet I have a feeling that there is an increasing number of people today more wedded to smash and grab for themselves and their immediate mates than to sacrificial service for those most in need.

All honour to the Royal College of Nursing whose members, despite a genuine grievance about their pay, still refuse to go on strike because their vocation is to serve the sick and not desert them. Of course people have a right to fight for reasonable standards of pay and conditions of work. But if you

are in a job which exists to serve your fellow men and women
(as most jobs claim to do), how can you lay aside the duty to
love your neighbour as yourself, how can you justify turning
the slogan of the Rotary Club 'service above self' topsy turvy
and proclaiming 'self before service'.

3 *The Legion's opportunity*

The Royal British Legion is one of the great serving voluntary
organizations which are so vital a part of our community life.
Many of the caring jobs (which have now rightly become
professional), such as medicine, social work, education, much
of the civil service, the care of the elderly and the very young
began as voluntary movements within the Christian Church.
It is a tragedy when the vocation to be of disinterested service
to others gets lost in the political and economic scramble for
power and status.

Can the Legion, with its thousands of members, help the
nation to strengthen that spirit of co-operation and service
which is in danger of being smothered in some areas of our life
together, but which is the life-blood of our Christian understanding of democracy.

Lay to heart those words of Jesus whom the disciples rightly
called Master, but who was himself happy to say 'I am among
you as one who serves'. (Luke 22.27) Only in that spirit—the
spirit of service and not smash and grab, the spirit of humility
and not pride, the spirit of give and not take—only in that
spirit can the pursuit of democracy and peace, so solemnly laid
upon members of the Royal British Legion by the late Earl
Mountbatten, take place. Only in that spirit can democracy
succeed and peace be given a chance.

10   LAW AND RIGHTEOUSNESS

at a service for members of the legal profession

*The traditional link between the Law and religion is
symbolized in cathedrals and the parish churches in major
cities when Her Majesty's judges attend an act of worship in
state at the start of a new law term. This valuable link can also*

be recognized in other places by inviting magistrates, solicitors, and others connected with the legal profession to a special service designed to carry on this important tradition. The preacher must avoid the temptation to pontificate on legal matters about which his congregation is likely to be much better informed than himself, but he can certainly find in the Bible many themes which he can usefully employ. This sermon examines the relationship between the law and religion in the light of the teachings of both Jeremiah and St Paul.

Of the many great discoveries which the Jewish people made about God and man, none was more profound nor more far-reaching than their insistence that there is an inextricable relationship between the enactment and enforcement of law on the one hand, and the worship of Almighty God on the other.

1 *The two great commandments*

At its simplest, this was summed up in the two-fold commandment to love the Lord your God with all your heart and mind and soul and strength, and to love your neighbour as yourself. In the more sophisticated regulations outlined in the great law books called Deuteronomy and Leviticus, there was no part of life which was not the subject of legal codes, and equally no part of life which was not seen in terms of obedience or disobedience to the divine will. Right conduct and righteousness were all of a piece. Throughout the Bible, in the Old Testament and the New, law and religion go hand in hand. Each was seen to be vitally necessary to the other. But the Victorian poet who optimistically believed that man must needs love the highest when he sees it, did not have either the evidence of history nor human experience to back him. For there is a deep-seated spirit of rebellion in all of us. When we see the injunction not to walk on the grass, our feet itch to do just that. The amber light on the traffic signals seems to be a sign to many motorists to accelerate. Punch once had a cartoon which brilliantly caught the feel of what theologians call original sin. It showed a vast field with nothing in it except a notice board on which nothing was written but the words 'It is forbidden to throw stones at this notice board'. I

34

used to think as a boy at school that most of the rules were invented by the masters for the sole purpose of seeing whether we would break them.

2 The limitations of law

Paul knew this only too well. *When I want to do right, only wrong is within my reach. The will to do good is there, the deed is not.* (Rom. 7.21) And this led him in another place to make the staggering admission *Sin gains its power from the law.* (1 Cor. 15.56)

All this suggests what should be obvious. It is that law, though essential to the conduct of our human affairs, yet has a very limited place in them. Law is there to protect the weak, and at times we all need that protection. Law is there to protect us from ourselves. But it cannot make us virtuous, and when law enters into the field of morality, it nearly always runs into difficulties. How far can matters of literary taste, sexual behaviour, or Sunday observance be dealt with by law, except in the limited sense of protecting the vulnerable? By the same token, talk about the imposition of harsher penalties, 'short sharp shocks', and more legislation in the name of 'law and order' can only make a very limited impact on the well-being of society, and may even prove to be counter-productive.

3 Jeremiah's vision

The Old Testament writers knew the importance of law, and many of them were brilliant legislators. But they also began to see that the point would be reached where something more than law was needed for the health of the community. It was Jeremiah, the most sensitive of the prophets, who, seven centuries before Christ, put these feelings into unforgettable language.

The time is coming, says the Lord, when I will make a new covenant with Israel and Judah. It will not be like the covenant I made with their forefathers when I took them by the hand and led them out of Egypt. Although they broke my covenant, I was patient with them, says the Lord. But this is the covenant that I will make with Israel after those days, says the Lord: I will set my law within them, and write it on their hearts. (Jer. 31.31–33)

We are here at one of the high points in the history of religious thought. Jeremiah did not wish to set the law aside, but he wanted to put it firmly in its religious context. He saw that the inner motivation which springs from the dimension which we call spiritual, and which finds its highest expression in worship must be more important and more effective than legal sanctions. That is why it is so perilous to neglect an appeal to the spiritual as so many of our leaders in politics, industry and social life seem to do. That is to ignore the motive power which can lift man out of the Catch-22 dilemma which Paul described when he spoke of sin gaining its power from the law.

I was deeply moved by the interview with Harold Macmillan on television the other night, when he pleaded that the dimension of the spirit should once again become apparent in our public affairs. He finished the interview on a note of high emotion when he described Polish trade-unionists working out their programme of freedom, within the restraints and complexities of life in a communist state, and working it out not only with their heads and hands, but also on their knees.

Jeremiah's promise is still valid. There is a new covenant to be written in the hearts of men. It is a covenant between man and his neighbour based firmly on a covenant between man and his God. And does this not still come as an intimate question to each one of us as it did when Jeremiah first wrote those words, especially to those whose religious faith and practice have grown dim or become a mere formality?

4 *A healthy society*

This service can itself be seen on two levels, the formal and the symbolic. On the formal level it represents the historical survival of a link between the establishment of the law and the establishment of the Church—a picturesque scene like the changing of the guard on the posters of the British Tourist Board. But on the symbolic level it points to what is, and always must be, a key to national survival: the deep conviction which comes over the centuries from writers both in the Old and New Testaments, that a healthy society demands not only sound laws respected by the people, but a living faith giving vision and courage and hope to a people who know not only how to be law-abiding, but also how to be righteous.

11   BABEL AND THE STRUGGLE FOR POWER

for United Nations Day

United Nations Day falls each year on 24 October. In most countries its observance is neglected or half-hearted, and little notice is taken of it in most churches in England. Yet it presents the preacher with a valuable opportunity for developing the biblical theme of the use and misuse of power, and exploring its relevance to the international struggle for power. This sermon was given in New York on United Nations Sunday, 1983.

I don't suppose that tomorrow will be a public holiday in New York, any more than it will be in London or Moscow or Tokyo—despite the fact that, years ago, the United Nations passed a solemn resolution stating that 24 October, United Nations Day, should be observed as a holiday in all member countries. In Liverpool Cathedral we held an annual United Nations Day service. It was just about the worst attended of the whole year, and we only kept it going because some of us thought it was important.

The truth is that there is much disillusionment about the United Nations Organization, and the reason is obvious. It seems as though the nations which like to call themselves the great powers are only willing to play ball *on their own terms* which means clinging tightly to the power they have managed to acquire for themselves and doing their best to frustrate anybody else who tries to overtake them in the power game. Meanwhile, the weaker nations, with a few exceptions, look on enviously at their more powerful neighbours and use what stratagems and alliances they can to get more power for themselves. Little wonder therefore that the power struggle leads to a succession of stalemates, while ordinary people despair.

37

1 *The Tower of Babel*

Has the Bible anything helpful to say about power, and the use of power? It has much to say, and much that is of importance to us.

I find it interesting to discover that just as the gods of the ancient Greeks got very up-tight when man first discovered for himself how to make fire, so the God of the ancient Jews seems to have been equally worried when man took to himself powers which might be properly thought to belong to God alone. Adam and Eve eat the forbidden fruit and God noticing that 'The man has become like one of us, knowing good from evil' is immediately alarmed, and asks himself: 'What if he reaches out his hand and takes of the fruit of the tree of life—and lives forever?' (Gen. 3.22)

And then just a few pages later on in Genesis, we find the strange story of the building of the skyscraper city called Babel. 'Come,' they said. 'Let us build ourselves a city and a tower with its top to the heavens and let us make a name for ourselves.' How does God react? God says: 'Now they have started to do this henceforward nothing they have in mind will be beyond their reach.' The consequence is confusion.

Strange how this folk-tale from the dim, distant past can set the theme for the whole Bible discussion about the use of power, how vividly—like a streak of lightning—it illuminates our own human predicament.

Let us build a city and a tower with its top to heaven. Do you see? Heaven is where God lives. Exalt the city high enough, and you can knock God off his perch. And in his place *make a name for ourselves*: political power—the power which comes from our science and technology, our business acumen, our economic skills, our nuclear stockpiling, even our chasing after success, or 'living standards' or sexual prowess. And in such a city called Babel, the talk is not of 'to God be the glory', but 'let's make a name for ourselves'. (Gen. 11.1–9)

The Bible warns us again and again what happens to nations, to families, to people when they put their trust in power divorced from all reference to God the giver of it. Godless power contains within itself the seeds of its own destruction.

38

History is littered with such ruins and is likely in future to be littered just as often. Here are some lines from a poem by Percy Bysshe Shelley:

I met a traveller from an antique land
Who said: Two vast and trunkless legs of stone
Stand in the desert. Near them, on the sand,
Half sunk, a shattered visage lies . . .
And on the pedestal these words appear
'My name is Ozymandias, king of kings:
Look on my works, ye Mighty, and despair!'
Nothing beside remains. Round the decay
Of that colossal wreck, boundless and bare
The lone and level sands stretch far away.

Some put their trust in chariots and some in horses, cries the Psalmist. *But we will remember the Lord our God.* (Ps. 20.7)

The Archbishop of Canterbury, Dr Runcie, and the Dean of St Paul's Cathedral in London, both got into trouble with some of our English politicians because at a national service of Thanksgiving following last year's Falkland Islands affair and our conflict with Argentina, they included in the service Robert Bridges' great hymn 'All my hope on God is founded', with this verse which particularly offended some of the politicians:

Pride of man and earthly glory
Sword and crown betray man's trust
What with care and toil he buildeth
Tower and temple fall to dust
But God's power, hour by hour
Is my temple and my tower.

'No,' said the politicians, 'We don't want to go to church to sing that kind of thing. We want *Onward Christian Soldiers!*'

It is too easy to stand up in a pulpit on a Sunday morning and feel safe in saying all this, protected from Madison Avenue by stained glass windows. Yet, when we take the Bible seriously and ask the sixty-four thousand dollar question: 'What do we mean when we talk about power used in reference to God?', don't you, like me, begin to have an uneasy feeling that this Christian gospel we confess implies a way of life which is clean contrary not only to the values by which many of our colleagues and neighbours live, but opposed to the whole framework of values of normal daily life?

3 *The Christian paradox*

On the first Sunday following the dropping of the nuclear bomb on Hiroshima, when newspapers in England were full of the new power man had unlocked from the atom, the collect in the Book of Common Prayer ran 'God, you declare your almighty power most chiefly by showing mercy and pity'.

Here is the Christian's paradox. For him the supreme symbol of power is neither nuclear weapon nor space shuttle, but a broken man dying on a cross. This is the supreme symbol of Love. The paradox here is so intense that some can only endure it by ignoring it altogether and making religion a totally private thing. Others resolve it by living lives of public or private dedication and self-surrender, like Mother Teresa and her Sisters immersed in the poverty of Calcutta's slums, or like those in monastic communities, wholly given up to prayer and contemplation. But most of us have to lead double lives, knowing full well that we are implicated in the structures and power struggles of this world, and yet daring to read our Bibles, daring to say our prayers, daring to come to Communion. We are bound to be compromised, because the philosophy of the cross as the symbol of ultimate meaning, that of self-sacrificing love, does not fit easily and comfortably into the way of life and the way of work our circumstances dictate to us. But if we want to lead Christian lives, we must not be afraid to acknowledge that we are all compromised. We must not mind looking foolish in the eyes of the worldly wise.

Do you remember what St Paul had to say to citizens of another great city: *To shame the wise, God has chosen what the world calls folly, and to shame the strong, God has chosen what the world calls weak. He has chosen things low and contemptible, mere nothings to overthrow the existing order.* (1 Cor. 1.27–29)

Does the cap fit us? It should.

I began this sermon by talking about the so-called 'great powers' in the United Nations. I must be honest with you. I must confess to you that I find it hard to know how to apply the Bible picture of power to the way that nations should

40

behave. When I talk to my friends in England who belong to the Campaign for Nuclear Disarmament, I have a sneaky suspicion that they have the Bible on their side. Then I think about it, and I can't quite bring myself to join them. And then I wonder whether this is because I am a coward, or whether I am muddle-headed, or simply because it is too difficult to find an easy solution. But I know as a Christian I have got to go on working at this, seriously trying to square the teaching of Jesus with the realities of the power struggle in a nuclear age, and knowing that I cannot just dismiss Jesus as an idealist and a dreamer. And I must pray that if I come to see the things more clearly, I will have the courage of my convictions, however foolish I may seem to other people.

In conclusion, it must be said that nations only behave on a world scale as we all do on a smaller and more personal scale. We can hardly be surprised at the way nations behave if we break solemn promises, if we jockey for power, if we tell lies or half-truths, if we are deliberately blind to someone else's point of view, if we give in to pride or lust or impatience or jealousy or envy as husbands and wives or parents and children, as colleagues at work, as neighbours in the street, even as neighbours in a church.

Can we learn to go against the tide by showing ourselves in our personal, family and social relationships, to be true disciples of God? I mean the God who declares his almighty power most chiefly in showing mercy and pity. Are we brave enough to stand out as true disciples of our Lord Jesus Christ, who showed us that the only hope for us and for our world will come by surrendering what we like to call power to his power, the power of the Cross, the symbol of love and the sacrificial cost of love?

Perhaps, like the people of Babel, we forget this, because we are too busy building our sophisticated towers, and making a name for ourselves.

41

for Thanksgiving Day in the United States

On the third Thursday in November each year citizens of the United States celebrate Thanksgiving Day. It is a great national holiday on which families and friends, with their guests, come together for a dinner of turkey and pumpkin pie in recollection of the gratitude felt by the Pilgrim Fathers on their arrival on the American continent over three and a half centuries ago. Churches of all traditions hold a special service on this day. This sermon was preached at a united service in which, for the first time, two neighbouring congregations, one Anglican, the other Presbyterian, shared together the sacrament of Holy Communion. This gave the occasion a special significance. Only four days earlier many millions of people had seen the first screening of the television film 'The Day After', which pictured the probable effect of a nuclear bomb dropped over an American city. The film had made a profound impact on many viewers in the United States and it had been much discussed in the churches. The memory of it was still very fresh in the minds of the congregation in Madison Avenue Presbyterian Church on that Thanksgiving Day 1983, and this could not be ignored in the address.

Although Thanksgiving Day is not celebrated in the United Kingdom, this theme of Thanksgiving in the perspective of the Eucharist could be suitably explored on many other occasions.

1 *National thanksgiving*

Everyone enjoys a celebration—a birthday, a baptism, a marriage, a wedding anniversary. When my wife and I reached official senior-citizen age, our children and grand-children got together to give us a terrific all-day celebration, with champagne and a cake like you've never seen, a day known ever afterwards in our family as 'the great geriatric party'.

And when the whole community finds cause to celebrate, it is even more exciting. When the Liverpool football team wins the national championship, as it often does, there is a triumphal procession all round the streets with the players in a motorcade, and thousands cheering, just as they did when

Pope John Paul II came to Liverpool—to the Episcopal Cathedral as well as the Roman Catholic. It felt good to be alive in the city on that day and you wondered why it couldn't be like that every day of the year.

I have been to the United States on a number of occasions, though never before on Thanksgiving. This festival stirs my imagination to roam over the length and breadth of this huge country of yours, and the miraculous diversity of people who are its citizens. There are millions of individuals celebrating their own domestic thanksgiving, but seen all together they make a symphony of gratitude, a nation-wide celebration of thrilling dimension. And within this great day of holiday, the people who call themselves Christians bring to the celebration a very special concept of thanksgiving because of the faith they share.

Another word for what we are doing this morning, as we celebrate Holy Communion together, is the Greek word Eucharist—which also means 'thanksgiving'. To this day when Greek meets Greek and one receives from the other a favour, he will say 'Eucharizo'—'Thank you'. Some Christian traditions call holding a communion service 'having a celebration'. So that, just as the families of America come together today for their special celebration with turkey and pumpkin pie in remembrance of the Pilgrim Fathers of 362 years ago, so we at the central point of our life as Christians celebrate with bread and wine in remembrance of the God who has created us and our world; the God who has redeemed us through the life, crucifixion and resurrection of Jesus Christ; and the God who, through his Holy Spirit, is the Lord and giver of life. The Holy Communion is thus our thanksgiving act, our essential celebration within the Body of Christ.

2 *Holy Communion*

It is an act of thanksgiving of staggering proportions and infinite depth of meaning. Every week more than 200 million people meet around the Lord's table in Holy Communion— probably the most numerous regular gathering of human beings around a common theme this world knows. A Roman Catholic theologian from Sri Lanka once said that if this act of thanksgiving could be vitalized into a true sacrament of

Communion, it would be the most effective means of bringing about that radical revolution which our Christian faith requires. This would not only bring that sense of freedom and responsibility which comes from personal fulfilment, but also the realization of those values of justice, truth, love, freedom, equality and peace which make up God's design for human society.

When we Christian people talk about Thanksgiving seen from God's perspective, we are on to a big thing. Soon in the sacramental prayer we shall be thanking God for the gift of life and for the world our home, and in token of this we shall offer up bread and wine. Gifts indeed, our own personal lives and the world in which we live. But they are gifts held in trust. We shall one day be called to give a solemn account of what we have done with our lives, and in what shape we shall hand on the world we have inherited to succeeding generations. Thanksgiving which is not wedded to a deep sense of responsibility under God can quickly become superficial, and dangerous.

The personal lives which God in his mercy has given us, and which the festival of Thanksgiving celebrates—our personalities, our relationships, our homes, our sexuality, our wealth, our families, our gifts and talents, our work, our faith, our church—all this, and more, is offered with the bread and wine for thanksgiving, for cleansing, for consecration, for service. *Here we offer and present unto thee ourselves, our souls and bodies*—if we have the courage to do so.

3 'The Day After'

Sunday's television film 'The Day After' was a solemn—though, I guess, far too soft—reminder that we are capable of making an unbelievable mess of this beautiful world, given to us by God to hand over intact and improved to future generations—if there are to be any future generations.

Last summer naturalists in Great Britain pronounced extinct an exquisite insect called the Large Blue Butterfly. The indiscriminate use of pesticides and the destruction of hedgerows by farmers in search of larger profits have destroyed the natural habitat of this lovely thing, together with other insects, birds, and flowers. This may seem unimportant

44

compared with the nuclear holocaust but both are symptoms of the same attitude. What are we to say to Almighty God, creator of all things visible and invisible when he asks us one day about this one, tiny, beautiful creature which he made with such loving care and we destroyed. What about the danger to the infinite variety of natural life in the sea from enormous oil slicks discharged from giant tankers, by taking dangerous short cuts in the pursuit of more money? What about the even greater threat from the nuclear waste dumped on the ocean floor, by governments who pretend it is not there? Or the despoliation of natural wilderness and forest to provide mountains of newsprint, much of which is thrown away without being read; or to satisfy the real estate developers for whom the demands of the shareholders outweigh the preservation of natural beauty?

We offer bread and wine to the Giver in thanksgiving, penitence and hope.

Thine the gold and thine the silver,
Thine the wealth of land and sea.
We are stewards of thy bounty,
Held in solemn trust to thee.

We offer bread and wine in thanksgiving. We also offer it in the name of the Giver who has called us to share in his feast with one another. *Take this, and divide it among yourselves*, says Jesus as he hands the apostles the plate and the cup. It is here as in gratitude we share the symbols of God's good gifts, that we know our need for one another, our need to join together in the adventure of making a world in which we acknowledge our common humanity as creatures, all of us, of the one God.

Yet, tragically, we celebrate Holy Communion within the context of a divided community—and we are scared to face the facts. In Liverpool the disintegration of our community reached boiling point two years ago, with a series of successive nights of serious street violence, when petrol bombs set buildings alight a few hundred yards away from the cathedral where I was the Dean, and the police retaliated for the first time in our country with CS gas. People asked each other, 'Can this be England—and now?' Only two days ago an Anglican Bishop from Zimbabwe in the heart of Africa drove from East side Manhattan to see what life was like in the

45

South Bronx. He was heard to say, 'Can this really be the United States?' And when I watched the depressing and sterile discussion by elder statesmen from Washington that followed last Sunday night's *Day After* movie, I felt despairingly, 'Is this really all that mankind can do?' They talked about missiles, they should have talked about people. When I think of Russia I think first, not of the Kremlin, but of a young student with whom I discussed for over an hour the poetry of T. S. Eliot as we rode together in a motor-boat on the river Dnieper in Kiev. I think of the members of a Baptist Church in Moscow with whom I discussed the Bible, and the crowded congregation with whom I shared the Sacrament in a cathedral in Leningrad. And when I think of America, it is not the Pentagon or the White House I see first in my mind's eye, but my many friends, both in New York and in many other parts of the Union, with whom I have worshipped and talked of the things of God and of man. So New York and Moscow, Leningrad and Cleveland and Buffalo, Kiev and Washington, become one experience in Christ. If for me there is one great cause for thanksgiving today—it is that.

4 *The celebration of love*

Is it not fear that paralyses us in the present international stalemate and in our own local communities, and does not Scripture teach us that there is only one antidote to fear, and that is love? And is not the bread and wine in this service the celebration of love—the love of God poured out into our hearts as we eat and drink the gifts with thanksgiving?

The marvel is that the Body of Christ (which is his Church) is spread today across the world, on every side of every political frontier and of every economic, cultural and social divide, as a sign that this is God's world, and we are God's children, and we are called to share and be thankful.

Forty years ago in a great rally in London's Albert Hall, at the height of the Second World War, Archbishop William Temple of Canterbury declared: *When worship is once again the consecration of all life, and when life itself—industry and commerce no less than family and friendship—is the expression of worship, then we shall see a Church fully alive, and the fulfilment of our social dreams.*

When we meet around the Lord's table, we talk of sacrificial

46

love, we share equally the symbols of God's gifts, none demanding a bigger piece of bread or a bigger drink of wine than his neighbours. Is this simply a form of ecclesiastical play acting, a sort of cafeteria for the pious, or is it genuinely the most powerful symbol known to man of the means by which we could recreate our political, economic, community and family life—and ourselves as human beings?

This is a question which demands the fullest attention that the Churches are able to give: *How are we to rediscover, not in the language of religion and piety, but in our daily lives, the real significance of the providence and purpose of God inherent in the Holy Communion offered for the whole community?* The Church must learn to look outwards, but the point from which such looking outwards must begin must surely be in that place where the Body of Christ is broken and the blood of Christ is poured out, the symbols of the inexpressible love of God waiting, in each generation, to be brought down to earth again.

And because we believe this to be true, as we meet on this holiday feastday around the Lord's table, we can feed on him in our hearts by faith with thanksgiving.

13   THIS UNIVERSAL THEATRE

to celebrate the birthday of William Shakespeare

Each year, on the Sunday nearest to Shakespeare's birthday, a special service is held in the parish church of Stratford-upon-Avon. Wreaths are laid on the poet's tomb, readings from his works are given by members of the Royal Shakespeare Company, prayers are said, special music is sung, and a Shakespeare sermon is preached. In preparing his address the preacher has to be aware of the particular nature of the congregation, which will include members of the Royal Shakespeare Company, playgoers, visitors from overseas, and people from the town and neighbourhood. The sermon must take the Shakespeare occasion seriously, but must also expound some aspect of the Christian faith and life. This sermon, given at the birthday celebrations in 1979, attempted to place the English drama, and Shakespeare, its supreme master, within

*the setting of the biblical understanding of God and man. But
sermons of this nature need not be restricted to the poet's
birthplace. Preaching with a Shakespearean theme might be
appropriate and effective whenever a production of one of his
plays can be seen either in a 'live' performance in the
neighbourhood, or on television. Many school children also
study Shakespeare for their 'O' or 'A' level examinations.*

1 The melancholy Jaques

I was at the Aldwych Theatre sometime during the past long
winter, catching a bit of premature spring seeing the Royal
Shakespeare Company's production of *As You Like It*. I mar-
velled at the skill with which the director set the scene and
built up our expectations for the 'Seven Ages of Man' solil-
oquy, and the magical way in which Emrys James delivered it.
But even more remarkable was the extraordinary silence in
which the speech was heard—and from an otherwise rather
cough-prone audience.

Why was the silence so profound? The production? Yes.
The acting? Certainly. But also, I guess, the audience sensed
that a purple passage was coming up, so felt they must be
quiet and reverent, as in church. As we went through the
seven ages—infant, schoolboy, lover, soldier, magistrate, old
age, dotage—I'm sure we were all saying inside ourselves:
'How true. How very true.' And feeling good and almost
religious because of it.

Yet I have a fancy that it is not Shakespeare who is talking
here, but his creation, the melancholy Jaques. Jaques, of
whom Hazlitt wrote 'He thinks—and does nothing. He is the
prince of philosophic idlers. His only passion is thought. He
sets no value on anything, but as it serves as food for
reflection.'

Unfair? I don't think so. For Jaques is, in fact, the arch
non-participator. Content to think of himself, in John Donne's
telling phrase, as an island, and not part of the mainland, he is
a detached observer who sees men and women as merely
players, sees them from outside.

Shakespeare, so all the evidence suggests, was not content
to sit, like Jaques, brooding on the touchline. He was totally
involved in the business of living, delighting to rub shoulders

with the sum total of humanity. Consequently, in the whole wide span of his breath-taking cycle of plays, he shows us, as no other artist in words ever has, man from within.

2 *The mirror up to nature*

Hamlet told the players—and here I feel, it is Shakespeare himself, the actor-dramatist, who is speaking—'The purpose of playing, whose end is both at the first and now, was and is, to hold, as 'twere, the mirror up to nature.' (And remember that, to the Elizabethan, this word 'nature', much narrowed in modern usage, meant the very essence of the human situation.) That is the purpose of drama—no less.

This is why Shakespeare's characters are so complex compared with those to be found in the general run of the comedy of humours or Elizabethan horror comics which fascinated his contemporaries, or in the comedy of manners which began to excite theatre audiences a century later. We derive immense enjoyment today from Ben Jonson, or Middleton, or Wycherley or Congreve. But they do not, to the same degree as Shakespeare does in *Hamlet* or *Richard II* or *The Tempest*, help us (in Wordsworth's phrase) 'to see into the life of things'.

I do not know whether Shakespeare was a Christian, though I doubt it—at least, in any orthodox sense of the word. Perhaps he was too much of a Renaissance man to be cramped by theological dogmatism, or too sensitively intelligent to be bothered with ecclesiastical niceties. Yet it is abundantly clear what a debt he owed to the religious view of man and his eternal destiny, the rich heritage of medieval Christian drama which was still a living tradition in the theatre in which he learned his craft. His approach to the problems of man owes as much to the down-to-earth biblicism of the Miracle Plays of the fifteenth and sixteenth centuries as to classical models.

3 *The farcical and the eternal*

Take a famous and obvious example—the *Second Shepherd's Play* from the Wakefield cycle. The shepherds are watching over their flocks by night. A sheep is missing. The finger of blame points to Mak, a notorious sheep-stealer and a shepherd himself. The indignant shepherds go off to his cottage in the hope of catching him red-handed. He hears them coming, puts the wretched sheep into his wife's bed, and claims that she has just given birth to a baby and mustn't be disturbed. The disbelieving shepherds enter and the so-called baby goes 'Baa'! There is a riotous rough house. Mak is tossed in a blanket again and again, until everybody lies down to sleep exhausted—to be woken by the angelic host proclaiming 'Glory to God' for Christ is born. With solemn faces, as if butter wouldn't melt in their mouths, the shepherds go off to Bethlehem to greet the new-born king. This is the farce of man's everyday experience played out within the context of eternity.

Or take Noah's wife in the plays about the Flood. She is shown as a music-hall shrew, the worse for the bottle, and henpecking her husband. And yet she, too, gets caught up with him into the great eternal drama of salvation. God comes to the rescue of all that is worth rescuing in mankind—even a drunken harridan married to a saint. The soldiers at the foot of the cross in many of these early Passion plays get the same treatment. They are a comical crazy gang going through their comedy routine whilst high above them hangs Jesus, dying for the sins of the whole world.

This is the tradition which Shakespeare, with his touch of genius, takes hold of and forges again and again into his plays. Bound up with the high drama of the rising fortunes of Henry IV is the world of Sir John Falstaff, of Mistress Quickly and of Doll Tearsheet. And it isn't only Clarence and Lancaster, Gloucester and Warwick, Westmorland and Surrey who go to the wars for the honour of their nation. It is also (though, admittedly, with the reluctance with which most sensible, ordinary people go to war) Mould, Shadow, Wart, Feeble and Bullcalf. That's how life is.

We used to be taught at school to think of the Fool in Lear and the Porter in Macbeth as 'comic relief'. And in a way, that's right. But there is much more to it. For the Fool in Shakespeare is the one character who is able to move freely in every circle. He holds together the farcical and the eternal. One moment he is bawdy and earthy, one of the boys. Next moment he is as wise as Socrates, one of the professors. And in another moment still he is facing us with our eternal destiny—one of the angels.

That is why David Essex as the clown Jesus in *Godspell* was more authentic to my mind than *Jesus Christ Superstar*, or Robert Powell in the TV spectacular. The David Essex clown spanned the whole dimension of man from low farce to high tragedy. Jesus himself must have done the same if he really was God made man—as we dare to claim.

4 *The immanent and the transcendent*

When theologians try to think about God, they come up against a very puzzling contradiction. In one way, they say, God must be so far removed from all human experience that all we can do is to speak of him in terms of hints and guesses. Transcendent, Mystical, Wholly Other. The *Via Negativa* of the Mystics—or of Eliot's *Four Quartets*. And yet that cannot be the whole story. God made us and made us for himself. The hairs of our head are numbered. So the transcendent, mystical God must be very close at hand, down to earth, immanent, incarnate, involved with us in our everyday comings and goings and doings.

Indeed, we try to reflect this in our ancient liturgies. Worship is sometimes magnificent, other-worldly, mystical, obscure, breathtaking, magical. Yet sometimes, in the simple prayer meeting, perhaps, or in the Salvation Army singalong, it can be homely, informal, colloquial, almost slapdash. This is also true of our theatre, with its deep roots in Christian tradition—from kitchen-sink drama and the debunking of the classics to what is magical, ethereal, remote, like the mystical ending of *The Tempest*.

All of this comes from a biblical tradition, so deeply embedded in English drama that you can find traces of it not only in the classics but even now in the theatre of our own time: in Eliot's *Family Reunion*, in Priestley's time dimension plays, in the groping conversation pieces of Samuel Beckett and Harold Pinter, in Peter Shaffer's *Equus* which takes us from life in the stable and life in the psychiatrist's consulting room to something about worship and eternal destiny.

The God who is high and lifted up, and whose throne fills the temple, is also the God who walked and talked with Abraham as a man walks and talks with a friend. I find this a recurring theme in the theatre. It is theology in totally

51

non-theological terms, holding the mirror up to nature, and to God.

And if the task of drama really is to hold the mirror up to nature, our nature reflected in the everyday farce of life, and yet reflected also in a reality beyond the transitory dimension of time and space—if this is truly what drama is about, has anyone achieved it with more perception and power than Shakespeare? In play after play he brings before us the whole panorama of humanity: saints and sinners, rich and poor, kings and clowns, preachers and prostitutes, lovers and haters, high-born and low-born, philosophers and fools, all of them created by God in his image to work out their divine destiny in what the Duke in *As You Like It* called 'this wide and universal theatre'—to work it out in the comedies and tragedies we all have to face in the changing scenes of life, as we make our way across the stage on the long road to our eternal destiny.

14   THE SACRAMENT OF MUSIC

at a festival service for musicians

This address was given in St Giles Cathedral, the High Kirk of Edinburgh, at a service to mark the centenary of the Incorporated Society of Musicians. The nature of the occasion clearly dictated the subject of the sermon. There are many other occasions of a more local nature when the preacher could take the opportunity of speaking about music in the service of religious faith. Of all the arts it is the one most associated with worship, and the increasing use of our churches for choral and orchestral concerts and for Music and Arts Festival services should provide many opportunities for sermons on this theme.

1 *A boyhood experience*

All of us, I suppose, can look back to some rare moment, or moments, in our lives when suddenly we saw things in sharper focus, or in a new light, or with a deeper understanding—so that life ever after that moment had a new perspective or a clearer meaning.

One such moment for me was in my early teens when the rector of my home parish down in Devon invited me to go with him to the Three Choirs Festival in Worcester. It was an exciting week for a schoolboy of my age, seeing in the flesh such great men as Ralph Vaughan Williams, Gustav Holst, William Walton, George Bernard Shaw and—a particular treat for me—Sir Walford Davies. I had heard his incomparable broadcasts on the BBC week by week for the best part of my thirteenth year, as I lay on my back with rheumatic fever. They had given me my first love for music.

The special moment that week was hearing for the first time a performance of the *Dream of Gerontius* with Elgar himself conducting. It was, for me, a total experience. The orchestra, the choir, the distinguished soloists, the expectant audience, the striking figure of Edward Elgar himself, and the September sun streaming through the stained-glass windows of Worcester Cathedral, so that the very pillars and vaulting became essential parts of the ecstasy.

With the closing pages of Elgar's score—the great cry of Gerontius 'Take me Away', the psalm of the souls in purgatory 'Lord thou hast been our refuge', the lovely voice of Muriel Brunskill in the Angel's Farewell, and the final return of 'Praise to the Holiest'—in all this I experienced for the first time in my life that sense of moving out of the dimension of time and space into what I have since come to believe to be a glimpse of eternity. The poet Wordsworth described it like this:

> *The motion of our human blood*
> *Almost suspended, we are laid asleep*
> *In body, and become a living soul*
> *And see into the life of things.*

I know *Gerontius* does not speak to everyone like that. But for me it did that September morning in Worcester, and still does.

2 *Matter and spirit*

When the last bars had died away, and I had come back to earth, I still remember the strange feeling it gave me to see that the means which had transported me into the heavens were just that very ordinary bunch of men and women who make up any orchestra and choir. There was the horn player

53

shaking out the saliva before putting his instrument back into its case. Those ladies who had so recently sung like angels, were now picking up their handbags and awkwardly lifting their long dresses so as not to trip over the precarious scaffolding which had provided their seating. I had discovered the strange mystery of the earth-bound roots of the experience which had lifted me up to the heavens.

William Temple, the great Archbishop of Canterbury, used to say that Christianity was the most materialistic of all religions. By that he meant that the Christian faith is not frightened of the physical, the earthy, the sweaty, because it holds to the belief that for humans like us, the nature of God is reflected supremely in the ordinary humanity of a man called Jesus. The two most characteristic acts by which Christians symbolize and make possible their relationship with God are Baptism and Holy Communion. When you remove the ecclesiastical trappings which surround them, these are nothing more than two everyday, physical, bodily acts: washing and having a meal.

When I was Dean of Liverpool I used to enjoy seeing our organist showing visitors behind the scenes of our mighty Willis organ, with its 9,700 pipes, its blowing chamber like the bowels of a giant ocean-going tanker, and the immense intricacy of its mechanism. And then he would ask them to sit and listen to this huge bag of technological tricks as he played one of the mystical pieces of Olivier Messiaen. Music like Christianity, is to do with the transformation of the material into the spiritual. But it is also to do with another mystery, the translation of the temporal into the eternal.

3 *Time and eternity*

The sleeve on the record I possess of Mozart's Piano Concerto No. 25 in C major, volunteers the information that the slow movement, the Andante, lasts for six minutes and seventeen seconds. This piece of information is totally irrelevant, except for programme planners and radio producers. For when you are absorbed in listening to music—or performing it—you are experiencing something which, though created in time and space, takes you beyond the boundaries of normal conscious existence. The sleeve may say that the movement lasts six

54

minutes and seventeen seconds, but you know that it opens
doors to eternity. As T. S. Eliot has written:

> Only by the form, the pattern
> Can words and music reach
> The stillness, as a Chinese jar still
> Moves perpetually in its stillness.
> Not the stillness of the violin, while the note lasts.
> Not that only, but the co-existence.
> Or say that the end precedes the beginning.
> And the end and the beginning were always there
> Before the beginning and after the end.
> And all is always now.

You have chosen to come to this famous High Kirk of St
Giles as part of your centenary meeting, and as it is Easter
Week, this service inevitably takes its place in this church's
celebration of the resurrection of Christ. Some of you, whilst
rejoicing in the inspiration and patronage which the Christian
Church has given to composers from Palestrina and Bach to
those represented in the music here this afternoon (Benjamin
Britten, Kenneth Leighton and Herbert Howells among
others), may nevertheless find it hard to accept all its teaching. You may have inherited or discovered for yourself a
religion or philosophy of life which you find more acceptable
than the one represented by this ancient building. Even those
of you who profess the Christian faith might, if you were to
compare notes, discover that you have reached a number of
different conclusions about the meaning of the risen Christ.

And why not? Each one of us is still a pilgrim, an explorer,
and none of us can dare to claim that he has reached the
destination of complete understanding.

We may find ourselves wrestling with the question of the
relationship between the Jesus of history, the Jesus who lived
and worked and taught and died in Palestine two thousand
years ago, and the Christ of Faith proclaimed in the *Te Deum*
we heard just now, *Thou art the King of Glory, O Christ, Thou art
the everlasting Son of the Father*. (And the relationship between
these two ideas is the major theological question the Christian
faith poses.) If you wonder how an earthly life of only some
thirty years' duration can possibly be spoken of in terms of the
Eternal Godhead, dare I say that the Andante in that Mozart

concerto provides us with a hint, to claim no more for it. It took Mozart so many hours, so many days to compose. It takes six minutes and seventeen seconds to perform. Yet, for millions of people who have given themselves to it as listeners in a kind of act of faith, it has opened a way to a reality which transcends the bounds of time and space into an experience which we might even call a sort of resurrection. I have always thought that theology can take us just so far in our exploration of God, but then a limit is reached. That is the point where experience must take over: the experience of love, of prayer, of poetry, of art, and of music.

T. S. Eliot, to turn to his *Four Quartets* once more, speaks of all this as the intersection of the timeless with time, which is, he says, the proper occupation of the saint. But most of us are not saints, and for most of us the vision of eternity is at best spasmodic. But sometimes we do catch a glimpse, like my first hearing of *Gerontius* half a century ago.

15   GIVE PEACE A CHANCE

at a service in memory of John Lennon

This was one of those 'special occasions' which present the preacher with an almost impossible task. John Lennon, assassinated in New York in December 1980, was a well-known native of Liverpool, and the Lord Mayor of the city suggested that a service in his memory should be held in the cathedral. As soon as it became known that this was being planned, there was a violent public reaction and an orchestrated attempt to have the event cancelled. Encouraged by the Lord Mayor, the cathedral authorities persisted with the arrange-ments, but decided that it might be more fitting to hold a Festival of Peace, using the words and music of Lennon, rather than a more traditional memorial service. The event was broadcast throughout Great Britain, and television and radio recordings were received in many countries throughout the world. The address had to meet a number of requirements. It had to be both brief and intelligible for the benefit of the large number (inside the cathedral and far beyond) not accustomed to listening to sermons. It had to give the reason for remembering

56

such a controversial figure as John Lennon in an act of worship. It had to acknowledge the good side of his character without glossing over the less acceptable aspects. It had to speak clearly about Jesus Christ and his death on a cross. This was no easy assignment, though correspondence received from as far afield as Papua New Guinea suggested that some people saw the point.

1 *Jesus and the 'way outs'*

As you may know, some people tried to stop us having this service. John Lennon, they said, was a bad influence on a whole generation, what with his drugs, his attitude to sex, and his disrespect for authority. I suspect they also didn't like him because he was successful, because he was rich, and because he was young.

But even if all they said of him was true, I still believe it is a right thing that we do here in this cathedral this afternoon. For this building is dedicated in honour of Jesus Christ who was always ready to side with the 'off-beat' and the 'way-out' as well as with the respectable and the orthodox. Jesus Christ, who seemed to be much more interested in the one sheep that was lost than with the comfortable ninety-nine in their cosy hymn-singing church. Jesus Christ, who said to religious leaders of his day when they were about to stone a wretched woman caught in the very act of adultery, 'Whoever among you who is without sin, may hurl the first stone at her'. (John 8.7)

This is the Jesus in whose name we meet today. And if it is true what John Lennon said about the Beatles being more popular in their day than Jesus Christ—and I think it may well have been true—this is not a judgement on the Beatles, but on the Christians who present Jesus to the world in such an unattractive light.

2 *Give peace a chance*

But, of course, there is more to it than that. We have deliberately called this a festival of peace, not a memorial service, because, at the time of his greatest influence, John Lennon voiced the abhorrence of millions of young people all over the world for the growth of violence of which the Vietnam war was a horrifying symbol. 'What we are saying,' he pleaded, 'is give peace a chance.'

What a fascinating time that was, when rock music was giving young people a responsible voice—a voice to say something of vital importance for the future of mankind.

All we are saying is—give peace a chance.

We have moved from that time, perhaps moved backwards. The era of flower power has given place to a greater aggressiveness—the era of punk. Young people stupidly dress up like neo-Nazis, apparently unaware that the Nazi period was responsible for untold misery, responsible for as great a concentration of wickedness as the world has ever seen. And today, as often as not, confrontation is the bandwagon to be on—and peace is given precious little chance.

3 *The cost of peace*

Of course in some ways, the flower power era was simplistic and sentimental. You don't build peace just by singing about it, or carrying flowers in a procession, or lighting candles, or floating away into a chemical paradise induced by drugs or alcohol. The peace movement must be made of sterner stuff than that. Peace is only born out of great cost, the cost of discipline, the cost of sacrifice.

Ask Martin Luther King, shot by an assassin's bullet in Memphis, Tennessee. Ask Dietrich Bonhoeffer, hung on a gallows in Hitler's concentration camp in Flossenburg. Ask Mother Teresa, slaving amongst the poorest of the poor in the slums of Calcutta. They gave peace a chance. But they had to give a whole lot besides.

John Lennon did not give his life for peace. He had it cruelly snatched away from him by an assassin's bullet. That fatal shot in the New York night reminds us of the senselessness of violence—and I don't just mean the violence of murderers and terrorists, but the violence of bureaucrats, or powermongers, of governments, and of those who use wealth, or colour, or sex, or politics, or class, or big business to get the better of other people. But if we are helped to see the wickedness of the misuse of power wherever and whenever it is misused, then that bullet outside the Manhattan apartment block on 9 December last year was not totally without meaning.

Strange that the central symbol of the Christian faith should be a cross, an instrument of violence. It might just as well have been a gallows, or a firing squad, or an electric chair, or a guillotine. Jesus took the Cross upon himself, willingly and with eyes wide open. He knew that to give peace a chance was worth everything, even the sacrifice of his life. Because that is the price of peace.

This is why that solemn Friday when they nailed Jesus Christ to a piece of wood, that Friday we commemorate in less than three weeks' time, is a Friday that Christians call Good.

16   THE CALL TO MINISTRY

at an Ordination

This address was given at an ordination of priests and deacons in Lincoln Cathedral in 1982. It is based on Paul's account of his own experience as a minister of the gospel (Phil. 3.10–16). These words offer inspiration and encouragement to all who are called to ministry in the Church, whether ordained or lay. There are many occasions when a sermon on ministry is appropriate, not only at the time of ordination, but also when a reader or lay minister is commissioned, or when a new incumbent arrives in the parish.

1 *'I press on'*

It is for me a continual source of astonishment and encouragement that St Paul, at the very height of his powers as missionary, teacher, theologian and administrator, could speak of his experience as something which he was only on the way to understanding. 'I do not,' he says, 'reckon to have got hold of it yet. All I can say is this: forgetting what is behind me and reaching out for what lies ahead, I press on towards the goal.' So the call to any task in the Church, whether ordained or lay, is not a call to a fixed role which can be precisely

59

delineated or perfectly defined. It is an invitation to exploration, a call to take part in a pilgrimage.

My final service as dean in Liverpool Cathedral last September was an ordination—on the forty-third anniversary of my own. As I watched those men and women receiving their commission from the bishop, I wondered how much they really understood of the task which lay ahead of them. I can now see how my own ordination all those years ago marked the start of my journey into the unknown.

I do not reckon to have got hold of it yet, but I press on.

This is the nature of vocation. I know that some candidates who come to ACCM selection conferences aim to give the impression that they have got it all worked out, that they are assuredly God's gift to the Church, and the Selectors had better recognize the fact. I always hoped that such men would be gently dissuaded from going forward until they had learned a little more humility.

Maybe some people really have got a hot line to heaven. Most of us have to cope with our vocations in a more earthy way. We believe that we have a call to ministry. We say our prayers. We talk it over with our friends. We test it out at a selection conference and during our training. An invitation comes to serve in a parish. More prayers follow. More discussion. But, in the end, it is our decision and ours alone. Even at that moment we may not be certain that we can yet say that it is all God's will. Probably only after many years, with the benefit of hindsight, will we find ourselves thinking as we look back on the pattern of our lives: 'This was the Lord's doing, and it is marvellous in our eyes.' (Ps. 118.23)

2 *The gift of the Spirit*

The gift of the Spirit is not the divine endorsement of an already completely worked out plan, the rubber stamping of a blueprint. It is the assurance of divine companionship on the unknown journey ahead. It is the invitation to a life of adventurous creativity, energized by the Creator Spirit himself.

There is a sense, of course, in which the ordination service does delineate the tasks assigned to the office of priest and deacon. Yet there is no such thing as an ecclesiastical identikit, except in the pages of a Wippell's catalogue. Each new ordination, whether of deacon, priest or bishop, marks a new experiment in ministry. The tasks set down in the ordination service only come alive as they find expression in the actual individual commissioned to perform them. And that individual is a compact of all the characteristics, experiences, training, background and personal history which makes him *him* and nobody else. Any concept of ministry which seeks to hide personality under the cloak of office, quickly substitutes magic for incarnation and officialdom for ministry. The Spirit of God is the Spirit of unity, and in ordination the gift of the Spirit unifies, harmonizes, marries the absolute uniqueness of *this* individual with the universality of the tasks he is called to perform. And it is this blending of the universal with the individual which gives to the ministry its dynamic quality. *I press on, hoping to take hold of that for which Christ once took hold of me.*

More than a dozen years ago that great Roman Catholic theologian Hans Küng came to Merseyside and was interviewed on the local radio. The conversation turned to the question of ministry and authority in the Church today, and what he said has stuck vividly in my memory. 'Authority,' he said, 'can no longer be allowed to rest on external title or office, but on an inner authority based on three things: personal quality, factual competence and partnership.' Or, to put it another way, authority such as you, now to be ordained, are given in this service, depends on the kind of person you are, how good you are at your job, and your ability to work creatively with other people.

3 *Life-style*

The duties of the various orders of ministry are laid down in the rule book. But they have to be fleshed out in the actual life-style of those called to minister. Many of the older concepts of clerical authority, appropriate to past ages, now only serve to paralyse. A dynamic Church is one in which those who are called in any way to exercise leadership amongst the pilgrim people of God must know that they, too, have to remain pilgrims, always seeking the gift of the liberating Spirit, which enables them to move forward in

61

competent and loving partnership with the whole people of God towards the goal set by Jesus Christ himself.

A dynamic ministry, fit for a forward-looking Church rather than for a backward-looking institution, can only be realized if those who are called to teach know that they must also be learners; those who are called to speak must also be listeners; and those who are called to lead must know themselves to be partners in ministry with the many other people amongst whom they work.

These are the gifts of the liberating Spirit which we pray may be poured out upon those to be ordained this morning, and upon us and the whole people of God as we press towards the goal, confident (I learned this many years ago from that great teaching bishop, George Cockin of Bristol) that the God who calls us and with whom we have to do, is the God who is on the side of that which is coming into being.

17   MOVING INTO UNITY

for the Week of Prayer for Christian Unity

The Week of Prayer for Christian Unity in January and the days between Ascension and Pentecost are amongst occasions in the year when the preacher has a duty to speak to his congregation about Christian unity. Not only do people need to be reminded of the biblical and theological reasons for the ecumenical movement. They also need information about the present situation and future prospects. That is what this address attempts to do.

1 *As it was*

This is the forty-fifth Week of Prayer for Christian Unity in which I have been involved since my ordination. This adds up to a lot of praying. Has it all been worth while? Have all these prayers done anything? The answer must be Yes and No.

Of course, a lot has happened. When I was a boy in Devon half a century ago, we Anglicans had precious little to do with the Free Churches, and nothing to do with the Roman Catholics. After all, we were the Established Church—the

62

Church of England. The Free Churches were definitely second class—their ministers not ever proper clergymen, we thought. Their people sat or crouched to say their prayers, unlike decent Anglicans, who knelt. They didn't even use proper wine at communion. As for the Roman Catholics, they were, we thought, a superstitious lot, with their priests muttering incantations and clanging bells, and their people not really understanding the ancient language in which it was all spoken.

What never occurred to us at the time was that the other churches were thinking just the same kinds of nasty things about us Anglicans. The Free Churches were thinking that we were a stuck-up lot. And the Roman Catholics saw us as a bogus lot who talked about being members of the Holy Catholic Church, but were really nothing of the sort.

2 *As it is*

What a marvellous change has come over the scene. Witness this service here tonight, and thousands like it up and down the country this week. Witness the fact that such changes have taken place in all our churches that if you switch on the service of Eucharist on a Sunday morning on Radio 4 and miss the announcement at the beginning, you will be hard put to tell whether you are hearing a Roman Catholic mass, Holy Communion from the Church of England Alternative Service Book or the new Methodist liturgy.

Witness the fact that the last time I observed the Week of Prayer for Christian Unity as Dean of Liverpool, members of my cathedral staff—my deaconess, three of my canons and myself—between us preached at all five masses in the Roman Catholic cathedral that week-end. In my own cathedral the Administrator of the Roman Catholic cathedral preached at both our main services, and at the morning Eucharist the Presbyterian Church of Scotland's minister shared with me in the celebration of the Sacrament, and his elders assisted in the administration.

Four months later, I had the privilege of welcoming the Pope to our Anglican cathedral to share in an act of worship for the feast of Pentecost with us and over 3,000 people from the non-Roman Catholic churches of Merseyside. The Pope then went on, accompanied by Anglican and Free Church leaders, to celebrate mass in his own cathedral. Yet I remember that when I was a vicar in this diocese in the late 1940s the Bishop of Bristol at that time doubted the value of a meeting for unity because the Roman Catholic Bishop of Clifton would not allow us to say the Lord's Prayer together. Thank God times have changed. All these weeks of prayer for Christian unity have not been wasted. Prayer has been answered in ways none of us could then imagine.

Still, in some ways we seem hardly to have moved at all. We are nicer to each other than before: more ready to meet to say our prayers together, and to come to know one another as fellow Christians. Yet when we are not meeting together, when it is not a special service, or week of prayer, when we go back to our synods and services and church life behind the closed doors of our denominations—has the ecumenical dimension changed things very much there? Or do we, on the whole, still carry on as if the others did not exist?

It is true that in 1972 the Presbyterians and Congregationalists joined to form the United Reformed Church. All honour to them. But in the same year two much larger Churches, the Methodists and the Church of England, failed to make it, and more recently the Covenant proposals which seemed so full of promise, broke down. Perhaps we were not ready for such an exciting step at national level. Roman Catholics and Baptists found it hard to accept some of the ideas put forward, and even between the other Free Churches and the Church of England there were problems. What exactly are bishops for was one, and whether they really matter all that much. Was a trustworthy relationship with one another possible when the Methodists and URC ordain women into their ministry whilst the Church of England (wrongly, I believe) still refuses to do so? Nor have there been any fundamental changes in the chances of unity between the Roman Catholic Church and the rest of us. That great Church still has difficulty in accepting our priests and ministers as true ministers of the Church, is still unhappy about mixed marriages even amongst committed Christians, and will not officially countenance intercommunion as a step towards unity, but only as something that can happen when unity is finally achieved. Non-Catholics for their part, wonder why Catholic priests may not marry if they want to, why the laity cannot be free to follow their own consciences in such matters as contraception, and why their Church is taking such a long time to make up its mind about joining the British Council of Churches.

3 *As it should be*

In all this, there are some very tough nuts to crack on all sides, and in all our churches.

The theologians of the different denominations are hard at it trying to sort things out and they are making some interesting progress, for example, in the important report of the Anglican–Roman Catholic International Commission. But it is not the theologians who are in the front line of the Church, nor even the bishops, moderators or chairmen. The major thrust towards Church unity must come from the Christian people who are in the front line: local congregations, parishes and neighbourhoods. It is there that after the failure of the Covenant the ecumenical movement must be got moving again.

This requires a greater sense of urgency amongst the ordinary men and women in our churches. We need a kind of ecclesiastical counterpart to the Greenham Common women, a groundswell of protest founded on the conviction that in our divided, materialistic and increasingly perilous world, the unity of Christian people proclaiming and living together the gospel of Jesus Christ is not a luxury, but an absolute necessity. Once you have felt the urgency of this, the urgency to be one with your fellow Christians, and felt it not just in your mind but in your guts, then you will be ready to take on a solemn question first asked over thirty years ago: 'Has not the time come when Christians in each locality should be doing everything together, except where deep differences of conviction still compel them to act separately?'

I would like to think that we have reached the point in our ecumenical journey when men and women, Roman Catholic, Free Church and Anglican could start meeting all over the country in quite small groups to come to grips with the great Church questions: the nature of ministry, our understanding of the sacraments, our use of the Bible, the ordination of women and the role of the laity in ministry and mission, and the great moral questions which continue to divide us. Much could be achieved by talking honestly with each other and listening patiently to each other, not content with surface argument, scoring points, or protecting prepared positions, but coming to know each other, to care about each other, to trust each other for the sake of the unity and mission of the Church, and in honour of its Lord.

Once we have reached this depth of commitment to Christ and through him, to one another, we shall find the pressure to live the missionary task together irresistible, and we shall be driven to explore new ways of sharing life together in Christ's family for the sake of God's world. And if this drives us to the very limits of what our separate traditions allow us to do together—and even pushes us a fraction beyond those limits, as many are finding themselves so pushed—it may cause some orthodox eyebrows to be raised, but it will make the movement move.

There can be no way forward without taking risks, though that is what always seems to make the Churches so frightened of going ahead. However hard we try, the future cannot be planned, only explored. That is what makes the life of the Christian so exciting, and so demanding. We do not belong to an institution, settled and fixed for all time. We are pilgrims on a march into the future. Part of that march is what we call the Ecumenical Movement. But it is of no use to God and man unless it moves, and in so doing is prepared to take risks. That is why we should, perhaps, have outside our churches a red warning notice: *Danger. Ecumenism at work!*

18   CHRISTIAN AID

for Christian Aid Week

The rapid growth of Christian Aid is one of the most remarkable and encouraging aspects of church life in Britain today. Christian Aid Week each May not only gives an opportunity for local churches to share in joint prayer and action. It also provides an important occasion for teaching an essential ingredient of Christian discipleship. As this sermon tries to point out, Christian Aid helps the churches to understand more clearly their mission in the world, and so to gain a better recognition of God's purpose for themselves.

Here we are on the eve of another Christian Aid Week, and some four million volunteers up and down the country are poised with seventeen million envelopes, ready for action on behalf of thirteen thousand local churches. Their action will be to help the poor, the oppressed, the homeless, the illiterate, the stricken, the persecuted, the underprivileged in our unequal and unjust world. And despite inflation, and our other economic difficulties, pray God that before this week is over, Christian Aid will have received more than five million pounds to bring to bear upon some of the world's hopeless situations.

1 *Two-way traffic*

Christian Aid is a two-way traffic. Who aids who? Obviously our house-to-house and church collections, our hunger lunches, our sponsored walks and all the rest do bring aid to the poor of the world. Yet I have a feeling that it is equally true, to say that it is the poor of the world who are helping us. In our comfortable and self-satisfied Churches we badly need another kind of aid, not to improve already high standards of living but to stretch our imaginations, horizons, compassion, generosity and love. And that's the help the poor of the world can give us.

By 'the poor' I mean all those to whom it is our privilege as well as our duty to send some small help through Christian Aid. I mean the seventy thousand Rwanda people, evicted from their homes in Uganda, urgently needing medicine, food, clothing and shelter. I mean people in war-torn Lebanon, irrespective of their faith. I mean the desperately needy in the rural poverty of Bangladesh, and the appalling slums of Calcutta. I mean the victims of typhoon disaster amongst the Vietnamese boat people, and of the brutalities of the Khmer Rouge regime. I mean the sufferers from acute poverty, revolutionary violence, and political oppression in El Salvador,

Guatemala and Nicaragua. I mean the sufferers from un-imaginable drought in Ethiopia and the Horn of Africa, whose skeleton figures are all too familiar from our television screens. I mean the people evicted from their homes by the South African Government in pursuance of its apartheid policy. I mean the eight hundred million of the world's inhabitants who live in absolute poverty.

These are the people to whom we send aid, and who, in return give us vision. The vision shows what the Church of Jesus Christ could be if it were truly loyal to the Master.

2 *A new vision*

Let me explain what I mean.

First, Christian Aid helps us to put caring firmly at the centre of the Church's life. Those millions in the Third World press and press on the dull nerve spots of our ecclesiastical consciousness, until we come to know that caring cannot be put to one side as a kind of optional extra to be undertaken when we have sung our hymns and said our prayers, been to church and attended synods, and done all the churchy, religious things we are supposed to do. These unknown millions of the world's poor remind us with absolute clarity that if caring is not at the heart of the Christian mission, Christ is not there either.

Second, it is the poor of the world who have brought us together from our separated churches here this evening. In the early days of Christian Aid, in the mid-1950s, I was Assistant General Secretary of the British Council of Churches. One of my jobs was to travel the country talking to chapters of clergy, ministers' fraternals and public meetings urging the formation of local councils of churches. It was an astonishingly difficult job. So many people didn't want to know. Evangelicals were worried lest they might have to mix with Christians whose view of the Bible would be less sound than they believed theirs to be. High Church Anglicans were anxious lest they might have to compromise their views on the meaning of priesthood or the presence of Christ in the Holy Communion. Baptists and Congregationalists were fearful of losing their precious independence and the heritage of the Reformation. And most of these people didn't like the idea of hobnobbing with

68

Quakers and the Salvation Army who didn't seem to bother about sacraments at all. And, of course, in those days, as far as we were concerned, the Roman Catholics weren't in our picture at all, nor we in theirs.

3 *The call of the poor*

Yet even in those days, when so many were unwilling to commit themselves to such a dangerous thing as membership of a local council of churches, the divided followers of Christ were nevertheless often ready to come together in response to the call of the poor through Christian Aid. In doing so, they made the marvellous discovery that each was separately trying to witness to the self-same Jesus Christ. Certainly in Liverpool, where I have been working for the past eighteen years, I have seen Christian Aid bringing Roman Catholics and Protestants together in a remarkable way. The annual United Service for Christian Aid week takes place in alternate years in the Anglican and Roman Catholic cathedrals.

It is a marvellous thing that starving, illiterate, diseased and frightened people in Africa, and India, in Latin America and in the Far East—people we shall never see—have done for us what we were unwilling to do for ourselves, bringing us together in unity of service to Christ and to our fellow men. Furthermore, the urgent need of these oppressed people brings us to a better understanding of God's plan for his Church and for his world. They help us to see that to take Christ's kind of caring seriously in this unfair world is to expose ourselves to the risk of challenging familiar political and social presuppositions, to the risk of hard rethinking and radical renewal.

Christian Aid, like the other relief and emergency organizations is a sign for all to see of the world's need. It is an effective sign. Thousands of people are helped each year because of it. Yet it remains only a sign—and a sign not only to the Churches, but to governments, to international agencies, to multinational business corporations, and to all who have power to help or hinder the fair distribution of the necessities of life, to help or hinder the hope of millions to live in peace and justice. In the end, no voluntary organization, however well-intentioned, can solve the problems which Christian Aid

69

highlights. This must be done through the policy decisions of governments, international finance, and world-wide business corporations. We are all involved in this, as voters, tax payers, as shareholders, and as creators of public opinion.

4 Active involvement

Christian Aid itself is a registered charity and is not allowed to enter directly into the political arena. But its work inevitably raises a host of acute political problems. That is why so many Christians in so many parts of the world are beginning to see that to side with the world's poor in the name of Christ is bound to involve them in political action for Christ's sake.

In the face of oppressive regimes in many parts of the world Christian leaders, like the Roman Catholic archbishop Helda Camara in South America or Bishop Desmond Tutu in Southern Africa, find themselves having to consider giving up long-cherished beliefs about obedience to the civil power. The logic of Christian discipleship seems to lead them to side with revolutionary movements rather than with the *status quo*. Thus Christian caring may take any of us on to dangerous and controversial ground. This should not surprise us. Jesus never offers his followers soft-soap security.

These are the things that we in the Churches here in Britain owe to those we try to help through Christian Aid:

● they have taught us that caring must be at the heart of our religion;

● they have taught us that caring must bring us together out of our divisions;

● they have taught us that any honest-to-God caring must in the end land us in the uncomfortable processes of risk and renewal.

And the marvellous thing is this: these three things— mission, unity and renewal are precisely what ecumenism is all about. Ecumenism is not just a matter of Christians of different churches being nice to one another when it suits them. Ecumenism is that amazing movement of the Spirit which is slowly but surely grabbing us in all the churches, making us realize the impossibility of fulfilling our mission unless we are bound together in unity in Christ's common task—making us realize that our separated and impoverished

70

Churches cannot become truly missionary and certainly cannot become truly united until they are ready to undergo that kind of radical renewal of life and outlook which must entail risk.

And, as if by a miracle, we are learning these great things about the nature and task of the Church, not so much perhaps from prelates and priests and ministers and synods and commissions, but from the pressure of God put upon us through those unknown millions in the Sahara, in Ethiopia, in South America and Kampuchea, in San Salvador and Poland, in Calcutta and Southern Africa, who challenge us in our comfortable pews to take Christ's kind of loving seriously, and, in taking it seriously, to discover ourselves.

19   CHRIST AND INDUSTRY

at an Industrial Sunday service

Many sermons give the impression that Christianity is a leisure-time activity, to be worked out in personal conduct and family and neighbourhood relationships. But the teaching of Jesus has an equally powerful message for the world of work, and this should have a place in the preaching syllabus of every church. Industrial Sunday, or special services linked with industrial mission or local industrial or commercial life, provide opportunities for preaching on this theme.

The concern which brings us together this evening is one which affects everybody. It is not just Christian people who are bothered about employment and unemployment, wages and standards of living, unions and management, working conditions and profits, Jews and Muslims, Hindus and Buddhists, Humanists, atheists and agnostics all worry about these things, too! And let's be honest enough to admit that many of the opinions we form on these things have little to do with our religion. We are influenced much more by our income group, by our style of living, by our family background, by our political and union affiliation, by our education and social class. Yet I can hardly stand here and make

71

extravagant claims that because I am a Christian I know all the answers. I do not even know half the questions.

What do we think we are doing here tonight with all this singing about Arkwright and Henry Ford, all this chat about inflation and just demands and pollution? Is there a Christian thing to be said—a really Christian thing, not just the jargon of the TUC or Transport House or Smith Square dressed up to sound religious? I think there is, and I want to pick out two ideas for brief treatment, two ideas which come from my understanding of Jesus Christ.

1 *On the side of the weak*

First, there is undoubted evidence that Jesus Christ, as a priority, sided himself with the weakest, the poorest, the ones who had no voice in the society of his time.

There is a great deal of talk just now about self-help. The old saying 'God helps those who help themselves' is much loved by those who have got there by helping themselves very successfully. Yet I think the text should run 'God helps those who help other people'. Put it this way. However necessary cuts may be (and I have no competence to argue about that), and however fairly Governments intend to distribute their cuts, it seems to be inevitable that the badly-off get worse off still. The Political Research Unit of York University reported only this week that the poverty trap has never been so inescapable. In the broader context, some countries are better off than others, and our own country is an affluent country by world standards. The gap between rich and poor nations grows wider every year, and the Brandt Report which power-fully drew the world's attention to this global disgrace has so far received scant recognition either from politicians, churches, industry or the unions.

Read the Gospels of Matthew, Mark, Luke. You can be left in no doubt where the sympathies and practical compassion of Jesus were most often directed: to the voiceless, to the weak, to those least able to help themselves.

2 *The struggle for power*

I watched bits and pieces on television of the recent political party and trade union conferences. In all of them, in different ways, the big battalions were seen to be jostling for power, block votes, standing ovations, carefully arranged agendas and resolutions with little chance for those unable to push to the front to make themselves heard. In this respect there is scant difference between right and left. It is part of the condition of our common humanity. We scramble to get advantage for ourselves or our group. This brings me to the second thing I want to say, coming out of my understanding of Jesus Christ.

It is about the dangers of power. It was in the industrial setting, according to the old Cain and Abel story in Genesis, that the power struggle began: the vegetable grower versus the animal herdsman. The quarrel was about differentials. For the first time in history, someone cried 'It isn't fair!' For the first time, someone cried: 'Am I my brother's keeper?' History's first murder took place on the shop floor. They were struggling for power. Ideologies exist which ferment and exploit struggle and confrontation wherever they detect it, as the surest means of getting their own way. This desire for power lurks in all of us. The violence of mass pickets is all of a piece with the bosses who throughout history have hired and fired and exploited at will.

3 *Christ the servant*

But in Coventry Cathedral the chapel put aside as the centre of the industrial mission and the place of prayer for industry, is called the Chapel of Christ the Servant. It is dedicated to the Lord who washed the feet of his disciples, an act of humility which was the prelude to the climax of his servant-hood, the sacrifice of himself for others on the Cross of Calvary.

According to Jesus, real power is the application of love, of practical caring. It is not the smash and grab which we associate with power, the clenched fist on the poster. For Jesus the standard of living did not matter half so much as the standard of loving, the standard of giving. That is why he was so sceptical and so critical of the wielders of power. Herod, Pilate, the Pharisees, the rulers of the Gentiles, were all holding on to the kind of power which always corrupts. I am not certain what all this means for industry, what practical application it has for management, for unions, for shop stewards, for supervisors, for the CBI and the TUC, for the chairmen of multinational corporations, and for government ministers.

It may be too idealistic, impossible, pie in the sky. But if it is, the same must be said about Jesus, and you have to ask what we are about having this service at all. Certainly it is not the job of the Church to tell industry how to run its business. The Church as an institution is not technically competent to do that.

4 *Two maxims*

But it is the job of the Church to lay down guidelines according to the mind of Christ, guidelines which can provide the context within which practical politics and economics and industrial relations can be worked out.

Here are two New Testament maxims which provide a firm basis for conduct in our industrial and political, social and family life: it is the weakest who should have first claim to our attention and care; and self-sacrifice, of groups as well as individuals, is more important for the common good than self-seeking. If we could discover how to take these seriously and practically, we might begin to find ourselves living in a very different kind of world from the one we are living in now—a world the New Testament calls the kingdom of God.

20   SAY IT WITH FLOWERS

for a flower festival

With the revival in recent years of interest in flower arranging, flower festivals in church have become increasingly popular. They attract large crowds and raise money for good causes. They usually conclude with a festival evensong or some other specially arranged service. The preacher is given the opportunity of focusing attention away from the worship of flowers or even the competitive spirit among the arrangers to some central theme of the Gospel. This address, given at the close of a successful festival in a small Wiltshire village church is a meditation on time and eternity.

To be honest with you, there is not much about flowers in the Bible. Jesus seems to have been more interested in people, and I think that the focus of his attention at a flower festival would have been more on the people who grew the flowers, the people who arranged them and the people who came to see them—rather than on the flowers themselves.

On those rare occasions when the Bible does talk about flowers, its emphasis seems to be divided between their beauty (*Solomon in all his glory was not clothed like one of these*), and their short life-span—here today, on the stove tomorrow. (Matt. 6.28–31)

The end of a flower festival has a certain sadness. However diligently the flowers are watered, and doctored, they do not last. So much skill, and imagination and hard work has been put into this festival, but in no time the flowers are all gone, just a memory—possibly captured in a few coloured snaps.

Flowers have often reminded the poets of the fleeting nature of our existence. Robert Herrick, the Devonshire country vicar of three hundred years ago, wrote this:

> *Fair daffodils, we weep to see*
> *You haste away so soon;*
> *As yet the early rising sun*
> *Has not attained his noon.*
> *Stay, stay*
> *Until the hasting day*
> *Has run*
> *But to the evensong;*
> *And, having prayed together, we*
> *Will go with you along.*

> *We have short time to stay, as you,*
> *We have as short a spring;*
> *As quick a growth to meet decay,*
> *As you, or anything.*
> *We die*
> *As your hours do, and dry*
> *Away*
> *Like to the summer's rain;*
> *Or as the pearls of morning's dew,*
> *Ne'er to be found again.*

75

Time is terribly precious—neither to be wasted nor taken for granted. If a flower festival reminds us of our allotted span, that is not a bad thing.

Still, it would not be much of a festival if that were all it had to tell us. No sight is more pathetic than a grave a week after a funeral when no one has bothered to take away the dead flowers. As St Paul put it: *If we only have hope in this life, we are of all people the most to be pitied.* (1 Cor. 15.19)

2 *Glimpses of eternity*

Flowers do not only tell us of the limited lifespan allotted to us. They also, for all their fleetingness, point to eternal life—the eternal life which Jesus taught us could begin now, even whilst we are here on earth. Robert Herrick wept to see the daffodils haste away so soon. The poet Wordsworth had a profounder vision. One day, as he walked through the fields of his beloved Lake District, he suddenly came across:

> *A host of golden daffodils;*
> *Beside the lake, beneath the trees,*
> *Fluttering and dancing in the breeze.*

His heart was uplifted at the sight—ten thousand of them, he said, with poetic exaggeration. Of course they did not last either. But the experience they gave the poet *did*. He goes on to describe how sitting alone in his cottage, years later, he would suddenly remember the sight of them and the deep experience they gave him.

> *For oft, when on my couch I lie*
> *In vacant or in pensive mood,*
> *They flash upon that inward eye*
> *Which is the bliss of solitude;*
> *And then my heart with pleasure fills,*
> *And dances with the daffodils.*

In another poem after he had been to the Wye valley and Tintern Abbey, Wordsworth described the mystical experience which the contemplation of nature gave him. He called it: *seeing into the life of things.*

3 *The ladder to heaven*

I wonder whether you know that experience when suddenly the veil seems to be drawn aside, and with a great feeling of

76

joy, exhilaration, contentment, you feel that you are making a leap out of time and space, and catching a glimpse of eternity. You may have felt it when seeing a beautiful garden, or by looking at one tiny flower. You may have got it from a lovely landscape, hearing a great piece of music, or sitting quietly under the soaring arches of some great cathedral. You may have got it from falling in love or being in love. These can all be ladders which lead us on the path to heaven, giving a deep-down feeling that we understand a little more clearly the meaning of life. And once this becomes part of your experience you are beginning to have an experience or prayer.

Flowers come and go—and so (for that matter) do most of the human experiences in which we look for inspiration. But we Christians believe that there is one absolutely reliable source from which we can continually draw vision, courage, inspiration, joy, guidance and delight. And that source is a person—Jesus Christ: Jesus whom we can meet whenever we are so minded because he has himself provided the means of doing it. We can all read the Bible and share in the worship, prayer and sacrament which we find in the fellowship of his body which is the Church.

I have always been a bit worried by that rather sentimental poem about being nearer to the heart of God in a garden than anywhere else on earth. This is partly because it is tough on the vast majority of mankind, who have no garden—surely they have no less chance of finding God?—and partly because there is no evidence as far as I know to show that gardeners are any more religious than anyone else.

Certainly I rejoice at the evidence of the beauty of God revealed (say) in the rhododendrons at Bowood and Westonbirt—revealed equally, I guess, by the wild flowers in the hedgerows. But the only reason I know that I am meeting God in these places is because I have begun to learn to recognize him through my study of the Bible, and through my regular participation in the worship and witness of the Church.

And that is why we need not feel sad that the flowers so painstakingly and imaginatively arranged in this church will soon be on the rubbish dump. For the church in which the festival has been held bears witness, generation after generation, to the beauty and truth and goodness of the God, revealed in Jesus Christ, who reigns above the changes and chances and passing fancies of our human existence—'the same yesterday, today and forever'.

21   BECOMING A NEIGHBOUR

for a service in support of Christian social work

The parable of the Good Samaritan provides an obvious theme for a service concerned to focus attention on the social work of the Church. But the use of a very familiar Bible text tempts the preacher to rely on well-worn material from his drawer of old sermons, with a consequent dulling effect on the congregation! The more familiar a passage of Scripture, the more it must be approached as if it were being studied for the first time. Besides attempting a fresh understanding of the meaning of 'neighbour', this address also includes a brief description of the commitment of the Church to social action. The congregation consisted largely of representatives from the parishes bringing their offerings for the work of the Diocesan Board of Social Welfare. It was important that they should be given informa- tion as well as inspiration.

1 *Who is my neighbour?*

It is marvellous how you can always discover something new about even the most familiar passages in the Bible. The story of the Good Samaritan, for instance asks: 'Which one do you think was neighbour to the man who fell into the hands of robbers?' That is the New English Bible translation. It follows the familiar Authorized Version: 'Which one was neighbour to the man who fell among thieves?' (Luke 10.25–36)

But if you turn to the Good News Bible, you will find an interesting difference: 'Which one of the three acted like a neighbour?' Not being much of a Greek scholar, I was puzzled why this difference should occur. But I found out the answer when I was in Stockholm Cathedral a month ago at its 700th anniversary celebrations, and the preacher, a distinguished Swedish New Testament scholar took this very passage for his text. He told us that the Greek word which Luke used ought

78

really to be translated 'Which one of the three *became* neighbour to the man who fell among thieves?'. He went on to explain that the Samaritan became a neighbour because he went to the man in trouble, cared about him, and did something practical to help him.

This was a new idea to me, and I found it very fascinating. It is by caring and doing that you *become* a neighbour. And that is what the Church's social work is all about. It is about *becoming* a neighbour.

Who is the equivalent today to the man the Samaritan went to help? Who is my neighbour now?

My neighbour is the family fraught with anxiety because of unemployment and the fear of redundancy. My neighbour is the battered wife. My neighbour is the couple whose marriage is on the verge of breaking up. My neighbour is the teenager hooked on drugs. My neighbour is the old lady frightened to go out from the house where she lives for fear of being mugged. My neighbour is the black school leaver who is even less likely to get a job than his white friend, because his face is black. My neighbour is the girl who has run away from home to the city's bright lights because she is at sixes-and-sevens with her parents. My neighbour is the severely handicapped child longing to belong to a home and family, condemned to remain in an institution, or hospital because no one has the courage and the compassion to adopt him. These are our neighbours calling out for our neighbourliness, for our caring and our action.

2 *Pioneers of care*

Long before the State (or indeed society at large) cared to show neighbourliness to those in trouble, the Christian Churches in this country were pioneering forms of social care. The Church of England Children's Society, Dr Barnado's, The National Children's Home were among the great initiators of compassionate and imaginative child care, and were inspired by the deeply Christian faith of their founders—the faith which still keeps them going. Josephine Butler, the remarkable wife of a headmaster of Liverpool College, devoted her keen intelligence and her abounding energy to rescuing and befriending prostitutes and the victims of sexual exploitation and crime. She was a pioneer in the

79

honourable history of Moral Welfare work in the Church of England. The Probation Service and the modern societies devoted to the care and rehabilitation of offenders originated in the evangelical prison-gate and police-court missions of the nineteenth century. The Marriage Guidance movement evolved from the work of a Presbyterian minister, Dr Herbert Gray and Dr David Mace, a Methodist minister. The Samaritans, now an international befriending organization for the suicidal and others in deep distress, was started by a Church of England priest, Prebendary Chad Varah. The Christian Church in this country has a proud record of care and good neighbourliness for which we can thank God.

But inevitably and rightly much of this work has now been taken over by the State. Rightly because the whole community must undertake responsibility for the needs of the whole community.

3 *The Welfare State*

It is fashionable these days to denigrate the Welfare State. When the social workers were on strike, people said it did not seem to make any difference. This was untrue. It caused immense hardship. All that Social Security does, other people say, is to dole out money to scroungers. Just at the moment this is thought to be a vote-catching political ploy. Why should scroungers benefit from tax payers' money? But it's worth remembering that if, perhaps, 3 million pounds a year is misspent because of 'social security scroungers', this is little compared with an estimated figure of 11,000 million pounds a year lost to the country by tax evasion.

Of course the system is not perfect—what system is?—but the Welfare State remains a credit to our country, and the envy of many. Hundreds of Christian men and women find a vocation to serve God by working within the state system. This is a department of our national life which should be spared the cuts in finance which the Government threatens to make.

But none of this relieves the Church itself, nor the individual Christians of whom the Church consists, from a continuing responsibility to display by compassionate action the neighbourliness to which Christ calls us all.

4 *Individual involvement*

The individual Christian has an obvious responsibility to keep a friendly eye on his neighbours, and without being nosey and interfering, to show friendship and care for the most vulnerable in the locality. This is something that everyone can do. But some can do more. They can offer that most precious of commodities—time. Increasingly both the State social services and the voluntary organizations are making use of volunteers in a wide variety of tasks to help families at risk. Driving people to hospital, or to visit relatives in prison; collecting and distributing furniture and clothes; visiting and getting to know people in need in their homes; assisting in play schemes; working with the handicapped—these are jobs we can do, and much more. Social workers are beginning to realize more and more that, with the heavy case-loads they now have to carry, they are unable to provide the necessary long-term caring service without the help of responsible and concerned voluntary workers. Perhaps this new partnership between professionals and volunteers is the single most significant and hopeful thing to have happened in recent years in the contemporary social welfare scene.

It is, then, the responsibility of the whole congregation to show itself a good neighbour to the community it serves. For the local church does not exist solely or even primarily for the enjoyment and inspiration of its own members. Practically everything we sing or say, speak or hear in church will fall to the ground if the congregation fails to demonstrate itself as a caring and welcoming community. And this caring ought to spill out into the surrounding area by such things as good neighbour and street warden schemes. A watchful and practical concern for the needs of the people who live around the parish church should find a continual place on the agenda of the parochial church council, the parish fellowship, the Mothers' Union, the Men's Society, and the youth club.

5 *The role of the Church*

At the centre of all this are the Church's own social workers whose names appear on your order of service. They are put there so that you may know who they are, get in touch with them if you can help them (or need their help), and so that you can remember them in your prayers. They are the Church's own trained and specialized agents in the field of social caring. They are the modern successors to Josephine Butler and the other pioneers, although their work inevitably changes with changing circumstances and social conditions. In essence, they are there because they are, in their own persons, living signs and symbols of the call of Christ to his whole Church to care.

In a little while the representatives of the parishes will go up to the high altar to present to the bishop the offering of their parishes for social work in this diocese. The money received will be used to supplement the still inadequate salaries our workers are paid. The Offertory Procession is a sign of the solidarity of the parishes with the workers, and a kind of guarantee of future support. Each individual Church member who walks in that procession represents all the other individual Christians in our parishes who are called to offer themselves as servants of Christ in the caring vocation which is ours through Baptism and Confirmation. Each envelope taken up bears the name of a parish, a sign that every parish should be a caring community. And as the bishop receives these gifts, he represents in himself the whole Church of Jesus Christ—Christ who calls each succeeding generation of faithful followers to discover afresh what it means to become a neighbour to all in need.

22 SERVICE AND UNITY

for a civic service

The ancient link in England between the Established Church and the civic authority is one to be welcomed and maintained whilst we remain sensitive to the ecumenical spirit of the times. The civic service held in many parish churches, generally at the start of a new municipal year, provides an opportunity for the celebration in thanksgiving, penitence and prayer for the well-being of the local community, and for the preacher to speak 'Thus saith the Lord' to the condition of local political

and community life. This sermon was preached in Liverpool at
a time when the city council was deeply divided and the office of
Lord Mayor was under threat. It has since been abolished.

1 *The office of Lord Mayor*

I have discovered in my eighteen years as Dean of Liverpool that sitting up here on St James' Mount provides an excellent opportunity for Lord Mayor watching. I have seen eighteen come and go in that office, and from this I have derived two overriding impressions. One is of the consistently high calibre of the men and women called by their fellow-citizens to fulfil this important role in the life of our city. The other is of my growing respect and admiration for the office of the Lord Mayoralty itself.

I am not myself given to nationalistic jingoism, and in many areas of life, other countries seem to me to do things better than we do. But my knowledge of chief citizens in the towns of their lands convinces me that in our ancient tradition of Lord Mayors and Mayors, we do better than most. To devalue this civic dignity, as some would have it, by abolishing the robes and chains of office, or by making the Lord Mayor do his rounds on a bicycle instead of in his official car, or by banning the modest hospitality offered in our uniquely beautiful town hall, would, in my view, be to lose, for the sake of small economies and in the name of a bogus egalitarianism, one of the few stabilizing influences in our volatile and erratic practice of local government. I believe this to be true for reasons which I think have good biblical foundation. Let me explain.

2 *Service and unity*

The Lord Mayor, whatever his own personal beliefs, stands for two components which are essential ingredients in what the New Testament calls the kingdom of God. Those two components are the spirit of service and the spirit of unity.

During his year of office the Lord Mayor is called upon to put himself unceasingly at the disposal of the community— presiding, inspecting, welcoming, opening, advising, listening, reconciling, encouraging, and bringing strength and recognition to that great army of organizations and individuals who themselves are motivated by the spirit of service to others. I dare to say that the Lord Mayor is deemed to be the chief citizen in our community because he is ready to be the chief servant of our community.

Put the spirit of service first; then the spirit of unity. In his non-political role, the Lord Mayor presides over, and seeks to bring unity to, the varied and conflicting elements which make up the City Council—by all accounts a more demanding task here in Liverpool than in some other local authorities. He also acts as a focal point for all sorts and conditions of organizations and individuals when he goes out on his journeys to visit them, or when they come to visit him in his Town Hall. There are times when he may be the only point of unity in our fragile and divided community.

Service, then, and unity are the two marks and the two objectives of the great civic office we are celebrating in this act of worship this morning.

3 The example of Jesus

Now turn to the New Testament, and you will see that these two things were also the marks and objectives of the life-work of Jesus.

The gospel makes it abundantly clear that, at the outset of his ministry, Jesus began, not by making speeches or issuing directives, but by giving service to others on a generous scale, bringing good news in absolutely practical terms to the sick of body and mind, to the despairing and the frightened, to the disadvantaged, the discriminated against, and the poor. So that when later John the Baptist sent a messenger from his prison cell to find whether Jesus really was the man with the expected message, Jesus answered 'Open your eyes. See the evidence of service all around you.' *Go and tell John what you have seen and heard: how the blind recover their sight, the lame walk, the lepers are made clean, the deaf hear, the dead are raised to life, the poor are hearing the good news.* (Luke 7.22–23) Later on he told his friends that he had come to live among them as a servant. Service is thus the first condition of the kingdom of God.

But the second condition follows hard upon it. Service must be offered in a spirit of unity and not of disunity, in the spirit of fellowship and not of rivalry. 'A kingdom divided against itself cannot stand,' said Jesus in one of his most pungent utterances. And again and again he used such vivid illustrations as the vine tree and its branches, to bring home the absolute necessity of unity for growth and stability.

The Christian Church came into being precisely to exemplify and promote the twin necessities of service and community. A church which is not at unity with itself, and committed to promoting unity in others, forfeits the very title deeds by which the New Testament would recognize it as a church.

It is a sad fact of history that from time to time and in every part, the Church has been more interested in serving itself than in serving others; and from time to time and in every part, the Church has been more interested in standing on its own dignity than in seeking unity with others, with the difficult demands of humility and sacrifice that involves. For these reasons the Church, despite its high calling to bring to the life of the community the twofold spirit of service and unity, has often failed—and has deserved to fail—to make much impact on the secular world around.

The Church cannot claim to advocate qualities which it has not been able to exemplify in its own life. Northern Ireland and Southern Africa provide two obvious examples of this kind of Christian impotence, and many more examples could be cited—including some much nearer home.

4 *The Church in the city*

Yet there are signs of hope. We have just been celebrating Christian Aid Week—in which churches of many denominations have joined together in a common concern for the urgent needs of the under-nourished, the illiterate, and the diseased majority of our fellow inhabitants of planet Earth. In Christian Aid service has pointed the way to unity.

Here in Liverpool our Church leaders have entered into a fellowship of mutual trust and respect, speaking to one another and listening to one another in Christian love, to a degree probably unique in this country. I believe they have been drawn together largely because together they have heard the call to serve the crying needs of our Merseyside community.

It is not long since Church leaders would be most likely to

85

boycott one another in any enterprise, just as some of our politicians still do. But there is a new spirit in the Church, the spirit of service and unity, the spirit of the kingdom of God, which gives the Church the right and the duty to say to the divided secular world 'Thus saith the Lord'.

Just as once in the Church (and sometimes still, God forgive us) denominational self-interest prevented service being freely offered to others, now it seems that party political and trade union self-interest still sometimes stand in the way of the best interests of the community as a whole. Just as once a preoccupation with the niceties of ecclesiastical orthodoxy kept (and still may keep, God forgive us) Christians out of communion with one another, so it seems that political dogmatism still prevents people of different persuasions from treating one another as fellow human beings, and as colleagues committed together in the cause of human need. And just as the Church has suffered grievously both in effectiveness and in reputation because its members have been divided from one another into denominations and sects, so too our community has suffered because of the divisions and tedious recriminations which disfigure much of our political, industrial and social life together.

Of course the solution is not simple. It is always easier to talk about these problems than to solve them. But Christians, at least, acknowledge the difficulties fairly and squarely by placing the Cross, the instrument of agonizing crucifixion, firmly at the centre of their hopes. As St Paul wrote to the people in Rome:

We know that the man we once were has been crucified with Christ, for the destruction of the sinful self, so that we may no longer be the slaves of sin. (Rom. 6.6)

In every sphere of life the true spirit of service and unity can only come about by nailing down self-interest and group interest and national interest, by crucifying self-assertion, pride of place, dogmatism, love of power, greed, and by substituting for these things—which the Bible calls death—a radical change of heart and direction. We must move right away from the normal patterns and priorities of the world, to that repentance and conversion and new life to which the Lord of the Church who is also the Lord of the world, continually calls us. It is not so much new policies which this world or this city needs. It is men and women renewed in commitment to service before self, and costly unity instead of easy division.

Thank God the office of the Lord Mayor in this city continually reminds us of this need for service and unity which should be the guideline of our common life together.

Thank God, too, that the Church of Jesus Christ still stands here within this city, proclaiming the Christ who points uniquely to these ideals of the kingdom of God, and who on the Cross impresses upon us the high and solemn price that has to be paid deep down within ourselves if, as we pray, the kingdom of God is to come on earth as it is already in Heaven.

23   RECIPE FOR A GOOD LIFE

at a school Founder's Day service

In spite of the increasing secularization of society, many schools (particularly those of ancient foundation) still choose to come to church to celebrate their Founder's Day or some other high day in the school calendar. These are usually 'best clothes occasions' when the discipline and behaviour of the pupils and the achievement of the school choir and orchestra appear to be designed primarily to impress the governors and parents, rather than to lead the congregation into a sincerely felt experience of worship of Almighty God. Under such circumstances it is not easy for the preacher to say something which will be both heard and worth hearing. A further problem is created by the wide age-range of those present, and by the in-built resistance of many of the pupils to 'pulpit talk'. On such occasions the preacher is tempted to resort to anecdotes and generalizations in the hope of raising some interest or even a smile, but without saying anything of importance. This sermon illustrates one possible solution. Its target is limited to the older and more intelligent pupils and to those who are trying to face life seriously, but who may not yet have accepted the Christian faith. The approach is thus pitched at a deliberately humanistic level on the surface, though this will be seen to be interwoven with the theology of Jesus. The fact that this address was printed in the school magazine and also used for discussion in the religious knowledge periods of some senior forms, suggests that material presented during the course of a school service may have a further usefulness in less formal settings.

1 *Education for what?*

If you go to Italy for a holiday or for study, one place you certainly should not miss is the little city of Urbino, high up in the Apennine mountains. It is a place of very great beauty, and the birth place of the painter Raphael, and, even more interesting, it is dominated by a castle in which, in the early fifteenth century, lived a remarkable man called Federigo da Montefeltro.

You can tell what a remarkable man he was if you go inside the castle and, having seen the splendid state rooms and banqueting hall and library, ask to see the little private study where he escaped from his political and military duties to think and work and be by himself. On the walls of that little room, you will see none of the great tapestries and pictures you find in the rest of the castle, but a whole series of intricate designs depicting all the things that interested him most—chemistry, natural history, mathematics, geometry, history, poetry, art, geography, anatomy, sport, astronomy, music and much else.

This was the period known in European history as the Renaissance, and Montefeltro, like his younger contemporary, Leonardo da Vinci, was a true Renaissance man. He was fascinated by every branch of learning and art, and desired not only to study and practise each one, but, if possible, to excel in them.

Nowadays, I suppose, knowledge has become so advanced and so specialized that the tendency in education is to compel the student to learn more and more about less and less as time goes on. At 'O' level even, and certainly at 'A' level, in the scholarship set and in the university, and later if you go on to do research, you will probably find yourself saying 'No' to a lot of things you might like to learn about, so that you can say 'Yes' to a few things you want to study in depth. We may, nowadays, even be suspicious of the all-rounder, the 'jack of

88

all trades' who, we say, is 'master of none'. Perhaps you cannot hope, even at this school, to produce a modern Renaissance person.

More's the pity! Short-sighted specialists—whether art students with no knowledge of what makes the world tick, or scientists who have forgotten (if they ever knew) that beauty and goodness matter every bit as much as truth—such lopsided people can be dangerous.

What then is the twentieth-century equivalent of the Renaissance person—the really educated person? For as good a definition as any, I would turn to a man who was an agnostic, a pacifist who marched in the early days of CND, who sometimes shocked people with his views on sex and politics, yet who at the end of his long life wrote a magnificent autobiography which he prefaced with a statement of faith which seems to me in many ways to sum up what it means to be really human. The man was Bertrand Russell, philosopher and mathematician. I quote from that preface:

Three passions, simple but overwhelmingly strong, have governed my life: the longing for love, the search for knowledge, and unbearable pity for the suffering of mankind.

I have sought love first because it brings ecstasy so great that I would have sacrificed my life for a few hours of joy.

I have wished to understand the hearts of men. I have wished to know why the stars shine. I have tried to apprehend the Pythagorean power by which number holds sway over flux. A little of this, but not much, I have achieved.

Love and knowledge, so far as they were possible, led me upwards towards the heavens. But always pity brought me back to earth. Echoes of cries of pain reverberate in my heart. Children in famine, helpless old people a hated burden to their sons, and the whole world of loneliness, poverty and pain, make a mockery of what human life should be. I long to alleviate the evil, but I cannot, and I too suffer.

So speaks Bertrand Russell, who said he did not believe in God. But I have to tell you that his magnificent recipe for a good life—the longing for love, the search for knowledge, pity for the sufferings of mankind—is also to be found in the teaching and lifestyle of Jesus Christ, and in the end Jesus spells it out better than Russell ever did.

2 *Love*

Love involves giving and receiving. It begins in the home, in marriage and the family, among husbands and wives, parents and children, boys and girls in love ... but it spreads out from there into the neighbourhood, the community, the nation, the world. It starts in the home, and in the family because that is where loving and being loved has first to be discovered. I wonder whether it worries you that you are growing up in a society in which the generation just ahead of you is making such a mess of loving that of every three marriages, one breaks up—and whether you do not see this as a tragic failure that your generation must put right, by refusing to play fast and loose with sex, with solemn promises, with other people's lives. Jesus refused to see loving in terms of smash and grab. He pointed to a cross as a symbol of the self-sacrifice and self-denial that is part and parcel of any loving worth having.

3 *Knowledge*

Next comes the search for knowledge. Jesus took this a stage further too. It is not just know-how we need. It is truth. You only have to listen to politicians arguing, especially at election time, or unions and management arguing, or to look at the huge propaganda machine which envelopes us, and much commercial rivalry, and public slanging matches from people who ought to know better ... to see how quickly truth can be dispensed with when it is more convenient that way, and how easily lies, and half-truths, and double-talk become the currency of self interest. Perhaps one of the reasons why so many people want to keep Jesus away from their business, or their marriage, or their politics, or their lives, is precisely because he dared to say 'I am the Truth', and that can make you feel very uncomfortable. Is it your hope that the next generation which this school gives to the adult world, will think it more important to be truthful than to be clever?

4 *Unbearable pity*

Then there is what Russell called the unbearable pity for the suffering of mankind. This is a call to be compassionate in a society in which pity seems sometimes to be in short supply.

In a recent book David Sheppard, the Bishop of Liverpool, has argued that the most obvious characteristic of the lifestyle of Jesus was his bias in favour of the poor, and that this must be the most obvious characteristic of the Christian man and woman. A positive discrimination in favour of the most vulnerable in our society.

I have recently retired from eighteen years working on Merseyside, and I know how the sense of desolation and lack of human dignity experienced by many of those living in the area known as Toxteth reached boiling-point in the riots of July 1981 because they thought nobody seemed to care about what was happening to them. When I saw buildings on fire a few hundred yards away from the cathedral where I was Dean, I was not surprised, or only surprised it had not happened five years earlier. I know that black school leavers in Liverpool and many other cities have a poorer chance even than white youngsters of getting a job just because they are black. And further afield, the gap widens between the rich minority of nations (that includes us), and the poor majority, who get poorer all the time.

The warnings about all this in the Brandt report are largely ignored by governments, by politicians seeking election, by commerce and industry, by all of us, I guess ... as if it did not matter that people starve in their millions. I hope that whatever skills you acquire whilst at school, and later on in higher education or in practical work experience, those skills of yours will be put in some way or another at the service of compassion for others, and not just for your own standard of living or enjoyment. I believe that our great educational institutions, amongst which this school has an honoured place, have an urgent responsibility to this country. They must provide people ready to put their trained minds and their warm hearts at the disposal of those in need in this unequal, unfair and often cruel world.

So there you are: love; truth; pity—the recipe for the fully human person. No longer in the sense of the far-ranging knowledge and omnicompetence possible for Federigo da Montefeltro, the Renaissance man, but in a sense which will be even more necessary in the twenty-first century when most of our familiar problems are likely still to be with us, either to be aggravated further or eventually solved by the huge technological advances opening up. Then, more than ever, our skills in micro-electronics, or biological control, or the new means of communication or the final conquest of space, or the growing dominance of satellites over the affairs of mankind, will matter less than our quality of life as persons, the giving and receiving of responsible love, the commitment to truth and to trust, and the priority we give to those who share our planet with us, and are most in need and at risk.

If education does not give to each generation these things, it does not deserve to be called education. It certainly could not be called Christian.

24   EXPANDING HORIZONS

for students at the beginning of a new academic year

At the beginning of each academic year thousands of students begin their course in universities, polytechnics, and colleges of higher education. Many of them are committed Christians, probably leaving home and their own familiar local church for the first time. What help can be given them at the start of a new adventure in which their faith and the moral standards in which they have been brought up may be severely put to the test? This address was given in the chapel of the University Chaplaincy in Manchester, but there are many churches close to centres of higher education where help of this kind would be welcome.

What is there that can usefully be said from a Christian point of view to students at the beginning of another academic year—and particularly to those who are here for the first time?

Obviously your time at the university or polytechnic should be a time of expanding horizons. New experiences can be expected: new experiences of truth; new experiences of moral decision; new experiences of friendship; new experiences of faith; new experiences of service and commitment. These experiences can either set you on the right path for life—or lead you hopelessly astray. It all depends on whether you face up to new experiences hopefully, or run away from them despairingly.

1 *New horizons of faith*

Faith, for example: there was a time when people wanted to draw a hard and fast line between those who trod the straight and narrow path of orthodoxy, and those who strayed into forbidden territories of heresy and theological deviation. By and large, we are much less keen to make such distinctions today. Isn't this thing called Christianity a whole bundle of richly varied responses to the challenge of the man called Jesus? And doesn't our imprisonment behind the bars labelled Protestant, Catholic, Evangelical, Radical and so on restrict our vision so that we fail to see the wide dimension of the Jesus experience. We are not asked to give up our convictions here, but we are asked to broaden our horizons.

There are not all that many committed Christians within student bodies such as that in Manchester. But there are enough to enable us to enter into the worship, the theology, the ethos, the faith, and the fellowship of denominations other than those with which we are already familiar. There is so much to give and receive from one another. The student Christian should be an ecumenical Christian.

Furthermore, there are bound to be new experiences of faith as it becomes tested in the context of secular studies. In view of the expanding horizons of knowledge, not only about the physical universe in which we live, but also of the influences which play upon the individual both from within himself and from the environment of his society, the things which we have already been taught to believe in our churches often sound naive and simplistic. Here again we must not run away, but engage in the struggle for the renovation of our faith in the light of new knowledge and insight. The Christian student must always be an explorer, and his exploration may sometimes take him into dark and difficult territory. A faith which is not put to severe test is hardly worth having.

2 *Moral decisions*

Then there is the experience of moral decision. During student years the pressures upon us to make moral choices come with increasing insistence. There are pressures to do with personal life-style. There are pressures to do with relationships with others—with those in authority, with our fellow students, with the wider community. The temptation is strong to go with the crowd, to accept the status quo, or to follow the whim of the moment. 'A man's conduct,' said Emerson, 'is the picture book of his creed.' Yet, when it comes to the crunch, how seldom we allow our Christian beliefs genuinely and powerfully to influence our everyday actions. This is where we need the support of our fellow Christians in the sharing of prayer, Bible study, honest discussion, and the give and take of friendship. Sex, parents, work, jobs, money, leisure—it is precisely in these familiar areas that Christians in the University are called to 'let their lights so shine', and to do so they desperately need the illumination which each can give to the other.

Yet in talking about sharing our understanding of faith, of worship, of moral adventure, I do not mean that our religion should be used as a kind of funk hole to which timid Christians escape to protect themselves from the harsher realities of student life—like those factory groups which meet at lunch-time to sing choruses, when they ought to be out and about in the canteen and at the trade union meeting.

3 *The risk of secular involvement*

The chaplaincy in a university must be seen not as an escape hatch, but as a launching platform for Christian involvement in those very areas where the university body is most vital and active. Of course, the plethora of political societies, pressure groups and good causes is overwhelming, and there is much touting for custom at the start of a new academic year. Is it to be anti-racism, or gay liberation, or the Conservatives, or Amnesty, or the Christian Union, or the Socialist Workers? The choice is endless, the slogans bewildering.

It is not for me to give guidance here—even if I were in a position to do so. Except to say that the Christian must, in my judgement, put his commitment to love his neighbour as himself to the test of secular involvement, even at the risk of misunderstanding and being misunderstood, and at the risk of getting his hands dirty. Where and how he will choose to work out his discipleship in the secular environment of university or

94

college must depend on himself, on his background, his temperament, and his experience to date. But there is no escaping the obligation to do so.

This kind of involvement must always be in the context of caring. Students playing at politics can so easily fall for the confrontation game, getting an immense kick out of bashing those with whom they do not happen to agree, whether left wing or right wing, homosexuals or heterosexuals, 'male chauvinists' or 'women's libbers', Marxists or Tories, black or white. Sometimes there must be confrontation in order to protect the weak, the disadvantaged and the discriminated against. But such confrontation must always be in the context of caring.

Best of all, when we can extricate ourselves from the superficial world of slogans and badges, is to show care and compassion in face-to-face service and encounter with those in greatest need. Such face-to-face service, in which we are always receivers as much as we are givers, provides essential stepping stones to greater spiritual maturity. And I guess that there is a third world calling out for such service here in Manchester no less than in Africa or Asia.

This leads me to my final point. Each new chapter in life offers the hope of fresh encounters with God. God, as a friend of mine was fond of insisting, is on the side of that which is coming into being.

You begin a new year here—perhaps you are embarking on it for the first time, with all the varied, unknown, exciting, challenging, bewildering experiences which lie ahead. If you will make them so, they will prove to be meeting points with the living God: tutors provided by him in his school of discipleship. Then, when the time comes to leave and begin another chapter in your life, you will have achieved through your time here a wider truth, a firmer conviction of moral decision-making, and a growing commitment to serve Christ through his people in his world. And you will testify that when you came to Manchester you not only came to collect a degree, but to encounter the God who is 'the same yesterday, today and forever' in the streets and corridors of this place.

25 HEALING AND WHOLENESS

at a service for members of the nursing profession

This address was given at a service which inaugurated the annual congress of the Royal College of Nursing in 1976. The congregation consisted of nurses from all over the country, together with others concerned with medicine and hospital administration. The major theme of the congress that year was 'The Violent Patient', and this is the reason for the opening paragraphs of the sermon which analyse violence as a last resort method of communication. The theme is then focused on St Paul's analogy of the body (I Corinthians 12.14–26) in which health is seen as the effective working together of the many different bodily parts, and disease as caused by the malfunction of individual organs which cause the whole body to be sick. Those who preach on the ministry of healing at, for example, services for doctors and nurses at St Luke's-tide, will find encouragement that the New Testament concept of healing as restoration to wholeness is increasingly finding a place in medical, psychiatric, and social work practice today.

1 *The language of violence*

When the Edward Bond play *Saved* was first performed at the Royal Court Theatre in London, it caused something of a sensation because it included one or two scenes of what some people thought to be unacceptable violence. Yet it was, in my judgement, not only very well written, but also a worthwhile dramatic venture in that it tried to take a serious look at a group of teenagers whose life style centred upon the related themes of sexual promiscuity and personal violence, and tried to give some serious analysis of this all-too-common situation. Here portrayed on the stage was a group of boys and girls, who seemed unable to communicate with one another or with society except through sexual and personal assault. There was a horrible and inexorable logic in the climax of the play when a baby gets killed in its pram in the course of a general affray when the group goes berserk and can do nothing but hurl stones and abuse. The clue—if clues are to be found in this strange phenomenon of teenage violence—is suggested in the last act when, for half an hour or more, we see this same group

96

of young people in the sitting room of one of their homes, idly flicking backwards and forwards through the pages of their comics. Very occasionally, they talk—if talking is the word— in monosyllables. They talk but say nothing.

It has been said that violence is the language of the unheard, and I believe that to be true. But the unheard are not just those who (like the youngsters in the play) are unable to communicate. They are also those who believe, rightly or wrongly, that they are not heard. In so far as strikes and go-slows and walk-outs are forms of violence, which I think they are, they can be seen as the language of those who believe that they have no other means of communication left to them.

2 *The ward sister*

There is no more vital issue for the well-being of society today than that of community and communication. How to speak to one another? How to listen to one another? How to be heard by one another? Whether it be management and labour, the old and the young, black and white, the governing and the governed—everywhere the problem is the same: how to speak; how to listen; how to be heard. Indeed, workers often feel that management is not listening. Blacks often feel that whites don't understand. The young often feel that the old don't want to understand. And when communication fails, trust fails. And when trust fails the body—whether that body is a factory, a neighbourhood, a school, a family, a political party or a hospital—that body becomes out of joint. It becomes diseased. And the elusive secret of communication has to be searched for all over again.

I remember an eminent consultant in Liverpool once telling me that if the pay of workers in the hospital service were to depend on the importance of the job they did, he would want to see the ward sister at the top of the league. When I asked him why, he said that it was the ward sister who, more than anyone else, was at the centre of communication in a hospital. She was the one stable link between patients, doctors, nurses and the whole host of others, not forgetting the friends and relatives. The patient needs to see himself within a lively network of communication: able to speak; able to listen; able

97

to be heard. There was a time when the patient commonly replied to the chaplain's cheerful 'How are you, Mrs Jones?' with the comment 'They don't tell you anything here'.

3 *The nature of disease*

Well, we are beginning to learn a little about the place of the environment, the place of the communication network in the therapeutic process. I suppose it is true to say that the discovery of antibiotics and such like, and the whole success story of immunology has helped to lay bare what may have been previously somewhat hidden. This is that a huge variety of diseases are caused neither by germs nor by viruses, and are cured neither by drugs nor surgery, because they are to do with a person as a person, and a person in society. It is not radiology or investigation in the theatre which will reveal the causes of many of these diseases (even though they may reveal the symptoms), but rather the careful analysis of the stresses and strains caused by an unsatisfactory work situation, by a disintegrating marriage, by an uncongenial neighbour. Such diseases have their roots in a breakdown in the network of relationships, in community failure, in the inability to speak, to listen or to be heard.

It is, I guess, not only important for the general practitioner beginning his diagnosis to say 'How are you?', he must also ask 'How's the family?' 'How's the job?' 'How's life?' Medical practice in this area is undergoing the same kind of revolution as is apparent in many other fields of human study—industry, government, family, neighbourhood, marriage. The persistent question in all these places is, 'What makes and breaks community—and so creates disease'.

I wonder sometimes whether there is ever such a thing as a purely medical problem, any more than there is a purely political problem, or industrial problem, or racial problem, or sexual problem, or religious problem. The human body is a marvellous complex of the physical and the personal. And the human person is part and parcel of society and his environment: *No man is an island*.

I suppose the nurse knows this better than anyone, for the nurse can observe the impact of the network of relationships which surround her patient, as consultants, housemen, cleaners, physiotherapists, social workers, chaplains, friends and relations come and go in the ward.

I find many of the insights of the Bible most illuminating here, amongst them the passage read as the first lesson just now. When St Paul went to Corinth he was deeply concerned about the divisions which were seriously disrupting the community life of the Church there. 'It has,' he said, 'become like a body diseased.' To put things back on course, he urged that the Christian community in that city should look at itself in terms of a human body. Wholeness or health is when every part of the body is co-ordinated, for the proper functioning of even the least important member matters for the well-being of the whole. Disfunction in one obscure part can upset the balance of the entire body: *A body is not a single organ, but many. Suppose the foot should say 'Because I am not a hand, I do not belong to the body', it does belong to the body none the less.* (1 Cor. 12.14)

We are beginning to realize that the social services cannot work in isolation from the community they exist to serve. The Welfare State becomes a delusion if welfare is seen as something that can be safely left to the professionals alone. Of course trained social workers are essential to welfare, and although they are often criticized, I believe that they do one of the most difficult of all jobs with great skill and responsibility. But the job of caring is the task of the whole community. The front line social workers are the neighbours next door. And if there were a greater sense of what voluntary service could mean, and a more urgent fostering of good neighbourliness, there would be fewer battered babies and fewer old people dying alone.

5 *Healing and wholeness*

Certainly healing, although it needs an immensely specialized, co-ordinated and highly skilled service, must also be closely linked with the wholeness of society itself. I suppose that, in the past, hospitals have tried to isolate themselves from the wider community. Doctors whispered amongst themselves so that neither the patient nor his relatives knew what was going on. Visiting hours were strictly limited, with the ward sister breathing a sigh of relief when she could tinkle her little bell and say 'Time's up'. All professions, whether doctors, nurses, teachers, social workers, politicians or clergy are frightened of non-professionals getting mixed up in their work. But professionalism can easily isolate, and by isolation lose the perspective or context within which the work is being done.

We need to broaden our concept of Juvenal's dictum: *Mens sana in corpore sano*—a sound mind in a sound body. We need to broaden it into 'a sound mind and body in a sound community'.

The Church has a role here in the healing process. At its best the Christian community has always provided a therapeutic environment for those who find the pace of life too hard for them. The Christian pastor may sometimes find the inevitable 'lame ducks' in his congregation both time-consuming and demanding, but he should nevertheless be thankful that they are there, and that they can find in the life of the Church the comfort and protection they so badly need.

6 *Vocation to care*

Furthermore, the caring ministry of the Church has always overflowed beyond the boundaries of the parish and the confines of its own membership. The first hospitals, the first schools, the first welfare organizations were all extensions of the concern of those who believed that to bear one another's burdens was to fulfil the law of Christ.

This Christ-inspired caring ministry does not come to a halt because healing is now the responsibility of the National Health Service, and welfare the task of the Social Services. The same divine command to bring wholeness and soundness to the divided body, both of the individual and of society, remains. That is why many nurses and many social workers still like to call their work a vocation, because in it they recognize a call from God. For them that call is to undergo professional training, and to combine loving care with maximum competence and skill. But for others there are different opportunities for voluntary and supportive service, opportunities which need to be developed and increased not only because financial cutbacks make the work of volunteers essential if much present caring work is to be maintained, but also because the health of the community itself demands in

100

many spheres that wholeness of caring which the creative partnership of the professional and the volunteer can bring.

But above all, religious motivation can bring to our concerns a philosophy of that responsible and responsive interdependence which we call by the name of love. Love declares that we are indeed members one of another, that whatever our particular and specialized function may be, we cannot do it in isolation, and that we have to order our lives and our relationships in such a way that, however, costly in imagination and sympathy, each and everyone with whom we have to do is able to speak, is able to hear, is able to be heard.

If violence is the language of the unheard, love is the language of those who both listen and are listened to.

26   SERVICE ABOVE SELF

at a Rotary Club thanksgiving service

From time to time bodies such as the local Rotary Club ask to come to church to celebrate some landmark in their history. This sermon was given at a service to mark the 75th anniversary of the founding of the Liverpool Rotary Club. The motto of Rotary International provided a useful starting point for an address which invited those present not only to thank God for the achievement of their organization, but also to resolve to take their terms of reference seriously, matching their words with deeds.

1 *Service above self*

This service invites a single theme: the theme of your famous motto 'Service above Self', to which already our hymns, prayers and readings have abundantly testified.

It is a remarkable motto, and rather terrifying. For both the Jewish law and the Christian ethic speak of our duty to love our neighbour *as* ourselves. Rotary sets its sights even higher. It bids you to love and serve your neighbour *above* yourself. God knows, I find it hard enough to serve my neighbour as myself. But to go beyond that—Francis of Assisi perhaps? or Martin Luther King? or Mother Teresa? or Jesus of Nazareth?

101

(And notice that with all of these a kind of crucifixion was always involved in their concept of service—a nailing down of personal self-seeking in order to be available to others.)

Rotarians belong to all faiths and to none. But you have chosen to celebrate your 75th birthday in a Christian church where the supreme symbol of your motto is seen as a body hanging on a cross. This is the eternal reminder that service to others in its true dimension is not just a little bit of kindness on the side, but a costly giving of oneself, a crucifixion of self-interest in order to liberate for self-giving.

The more I think about the world in which we live, the more I can see that self-interest is the great disease which afflicts us all. It is the disease which the Bible calls sin. And it is a hard nut to crack. Just suppose that your motto were to be taken really seriously both by individuals and by the groups to which individuals belong: by politicians, industrialists, trade unionists, managers, church leaders, devoted to service above party, service above union, service above business, service above church, service above nation, as well as service above personal self-interest and advancement. Would this not mark the beginning of the biggest revolution our society has ever known?

2 *The reality of sin*

I am not saying that we are not all decent men and women here this afternoon. I am sure we are, prepared to lend a hand in need, and to subscribe to a good cause when asked to do so. Rotarians have that kind of reputation, and thank God for it. But, in spite of this, are we not all caught up, willy nilly, in structures of self-seeking from which we are hard put to extricate ourselves?

'All have sinned,' said St Paul in a moment of stark truth, 'all have come short of the glory of God.' (Rom. 3.23) And remember, sin is not primarily a matter of a drop too much to drink every now and again, or an obscene word on the football terraces, or a surreptitious glance at a sexy novel or girlie magazine. Sin is our entanglement in the *structures* of self-seeking. Sin is a hunger for power for its own sake. Sin is the idolatry of success and the cult of popularity.

That is why to take 'Service above Self' seriously required

102

what the New Testament calls 'repentance'—a change of direction. It requires some overruling faith, or philosophy of life or spiritual dimension such as the Jews find in the providence and law of God, and Christians find in the life and teaching of their crucified Lord. It requires such a willing sacrifice of self and sectional interests and at such a cost, that few have dared go the whole way.

But at least we can make a start. During the seventy-five years the Rotary Club has been in existence men from many walks of life have grouped together in every part of the free world. They have met week by week in friendly fellowship, pledged to the maintainance of high ethical standards in their businesses and professions, pledged to see their means of livelihood and their position in the community as an opportunity for service, and pledged to apply these ideals in an international as well as a national and local context.

3 *The opportunity before us*

This is the Rotary Club, and for such a movement to have taken such powerful root in so many places in this twentieth century is something of a miracle for which we rightly thank God today.

Yet I suppose it is true to say that the full potential of your famous movement has yet to be explored. It was G. K. Chesterton who once said about Christianity itself that it was not that it had been tried and found wanting, but that it had not been tried.

Suppose 'Service above Self' really was the philosophy which guided all political parties, would not much of the idiotic shadow boxing which inhibits sensible progress in local and national government be done away with? Suppose 'Service above Self' really inspired all parties in our industrial relations, would not much of the ritual dancing between management and labour be seen as a silly waste of time, and would not unity be born from a shared desire to serve the whole community rather than this or that vested interest? Suppose 'Service above Self' really informed our social life, would we not find our present inequalities intolerable and our deep-down racial prejudices a scandal? Suppose 'Service above Self' was writ large over every ecclesiastical synod,

103

might not the divided churches become more impatient to sweep aside denominational self-interest in pursuit of the task they must share together? And if 'Service above Self' really could become the philosophy of nations, would we not struggle with all our might until the United Nations ceased to be a forum for self-interested nationalism, and became, as it was always intended to be, a workshop for peace and justice among the peoples of the world?

This is a great vision. But what hope is there that Rotary International, or, indeed, the Christian Church itself, can make any real impact on the appalling problems now facing the world in these last few years of the twentieth century?

4 *Ideas have legs*

Small beginnings can lead to great things. The Jewish faith sees its origins when Abraham and his family left a decaying civilization in search of a new way of life. And the Christian Church sees its origins in just eleven men who, with all the odds stacked against them, were on fire with a revolutionary message.

'Ideas have legs', someone once wrote. And Rotary has powerful enough ideas, as you will soon be reminded when your District Governor reads to you your aims and objects. These powerful ideas of yours are precisely what this sick world so badly needs: service, integrity, comradeship, compassion, true internationalism. Rotary is right on target—on paper.

But ideas must have legs. They must get moving. They must move off the printed page and the membership book into men's minds. They must be thought about and thought through until they become a programme for the radical reappraisal of the values by which our society and our world choose to live, to be translated into action in the vital affairs of business, commerce, education, politics, family, society, and religion in which Rotarians are, day by day, intimately involved.

And who can say what a difference that might make in another seventy-five years' time? We shall not be there to see it, but our great-grandchildren will. Pray God that their world will be a better one than ours, better, perhaps, because we have passed this way before them.

104

Perhaps even better because we actually meant what we said when earlier in this service we put ourselves firmly into the hands of God as we prayed him to teach us:

To give and not to count the cost;
To fight and not to heed the wounds;
To labour and not to ask for any reward
Save that of knowing that we do God's will.

27   **THINGS OLD AND NEW**

at a service for senior citizens

> *The occasion for this sermon was a service to which members of pensioners' clubs and other senior citizens were invited. It was held in Chester Cathedral, and provided a happy afternoon out for those who came. The mayor of the city as well as other local officials and clergy of various denominations were there to welcome them. A reasonably short address was required, and one that did not make too many demands on the listeners, some of whom were frail and of advanced years. The biblical message in the closing paragraphs was intended to provide hope and encouragement, and to support the Christian message which this service clearly conveyed through the simple prayers which were said and the well-loved hymns which were sung and enjoyed.*

1 *An adventurous octogenarian*

When, some thirty years ago, I was vicar of a parish on the outskirts of Bristol, one of the leading members of my congregation was a lady who was getting on for eighty. She had lived in the parish all her life, and she remembered with great accuracy what life was like in the village and its parish church well over half a century ago. I do not know how many vicars she had seen come and go, but I sometimes had the impression that she thought I was not a patch on some of those who had been there before me. Still I loved going to see her, and to hear her impression of days gone by, and what she thought of life today in comparison.

Yet, for all that, she was not content simply to live in the past. Far from it! From her mid-seventies she made up her mind that as each birthday came along she would try to do something which she had never done in her life before.

So when she was approaching her eightieth birthday, she planned (would you believe it?) to go up for the first time in a glider! She did not dare tell her married daughter or any of her family what she intended to do. She knew they would try to stop her by saying 'Mother, you can't do that—not at your age'. So she kept it a secret, asking her friends and relations not to call on her or telephone her at the cottage (where she lived alone) on the morning of her birthday. 'You see,' she said 'I'll have to rest all morning to get up strength for my eightieth birthday party in the afternoon.' They little knew that she had, in fact, got up rather earlier than usual that morning to go to the nearest airfield, where she'd had the time of her life riding in a glider.

Only at the birthday tea party that afternoon did this eighty-year-old, with many a chuckle, tell her family what she had been doing that morning. 'It was a wonderful experience,' she said, and added, 'I wonder what I'll be doing next birthday when I am eighty-one.'

2 *The wise householder*

That is the way to live, enjoying the memories of the past and the adventure of the present. Do you remember what Jesus said about the wise householder. 'He is the man,' he said, 'who takes both old things and new things out of his store room. (Matt. 13.52) Those who only live in the past quickly become bores to other people and eventually to themselves. Those who only live in the present can easily become shallow, because they are pulling up the roots of the past which are there to nourish both the present and the future.

I myself am not keen on the modern habit of putting everyone into pigeon holes, labelling some 'youth', some 'senior citizens', some 'handicapped', some 'black', some 'white'. Most people want to be treated just as people, with no labels attached. We are all human beings, whatever our age, sex, colour or physical condition. We do not want to be patronized or pampered whether we are young or old. When

106

my mother-in-law, who was still very intelligent and talented in her late eighties, had a spell in hospital, following a slight stroke, it took her longer to recover from the shock of being treated as if she were a silly old woman by the young and inexperienced nurses than it did from the illness which took her into hospital in the first place. She just wanted to be treated as a person.

I have been into pensioners' clubs where the elderly people there were every bit as capable of providing the entertainment and the hospitality as those who came (kindly enough) to do it for them. But the elderly were expected to sit tight in their chairs whilst they were being 'done good to'. They were being treated as a species known as 'old folk', and not as people.

3 *Memories of the past*

Every age has its own particular contribution to bring to life, and the particular contribution which the elderly have to bring is memory. I do not mean memory for things in the immediate past and present. That often becomes curiously unreliable with advancing years. I mean memory of the distant past, which often gets clearer as the years go by. Memories of over half a century ago, when life was very different, are part of living history. Younger people miss so much by not listening to the old. When my mother-in-law died at the age of ninety-four, I felt that there was much more I could have learned from her if I had found more time to sit down beside her and listen. There are so many valuable old treasures in the storehouse of memory.

4 *Fresh adventure*

But this must be balanced by attempting things which are new, like that eighty-year-old in her glider in my Bristol parish. I have met many elderly people who have found a new lease of life in their late sixties and seventies (or even older) because they have taken up painting for the first time, or pottery, or drama, or music or much else, and have discovered the eternal thrill of being able to say 'I never knew I could do it'. That is why the best organizations for elderly people (or for anyone else) are those which create opportunities for new adventures and fresh experiences.

This should be the pattern throughout life, taking out of the storehouse things both old and new.

I love the hymn we sang just now: *Through all the changing scenes of life, in trouble and in joy.* My parents had it at their wedding (though I was not there). It was sung at my own christening, though I do not remember that either, as I was only a few weeks old. But I do remember singing it at my own wedding, and at my sister's wedding, and at the funerals of both my father and mother.

> *Through all the changing scenes of life,*
> *In trouble and in joy,*
> *The praises of my God shall still*
> *My heart and tongue employ.*

We should rejoice in the past, the present and the future. Whatever changes take place—and you have seen great changes, both in your own life and in that of your family, and in the life of society around you—God remains the same. And although he remains the same, our hope is that as we go through life, our knowledge of him and our trust of him and our love for him will grow stronger and stronger. *God*, says the Bible *is the same yesterday and today and forever.* (Heb. 13.8)

We know about God yesterday because we can see him reflected in the life of Jesus of Nazareth. We know about God today because we can read our Bibles and say our prayers and join in the worship of the living God with our fellow Christians. We know about God forever because we believe that he has called us to meet him face to face in the experience which we call death, but which a great modern saint more fittingly dared to call 'the last great festival on the road to freedom'.

28   GOD, MONEY, AND YOU

at a service for bank employees

It has been the custom for a number of regional offices of some of the high street banks to invite their employees to come to a church on a weekday after office hours for a short service of thanksgiving and dedication. This address was given to a congregation of men and women employed by Lloyds Bank in the North West region of England.

1 The architecture of banking

We hear a great deal about the architects of cathedrals, universities and city halls. But we don't—at least the ordinary general public don't—hear much about people who design banks. Yet banks are likely to be amongst the most fascinating and impressive buildings in any city or town. For instance the place where my modest resources are housed is for all the world built like a classical temple. It is elegant, lofty, and made of marble. You feel a sense of awe and mystery as soon as you enter its impressive doors. It is decorated throughout with the signs of the Zodiac, as if to remind you of the unseen powers which influence the fluctuations in our dividends.

It is curious what an ecclesiastical feel banks seem to hold for the uninitiated, almost as if they were sacred buildings. Each day on my way to the cathedral I pass a drive-in bank. But I have never seen anyone drive into it. Indeed I myself would no more dream of driving into a bank than I would driving into this parish church. If, when on holiday, I go into a bank dressed in my shorts and open-neck shirt, I feel painfully ill at ease. It just doesn't seem right; for banks are 'best clothes' places just as churches are. That is why at no time would I raise my voice above the subdued tones considered proper both for banks and churches. Of course when 3.30 p.m. comes and the doors are shut against the general public, it may be all very different. I can speak only of what I see as a customer during hours of public business.

Why this church-like atmosphere? It would be easy to say that it is because people have made a God of money, so that they approach the vaults where the gold is kept with something of the same awe as Catholics approach the Tabernacle where the reserved Sacrament is lodged.

It would be easy to come to this conclusion, but I do not think it is right. It has more to do with the intensely personal view that most people take of their money matters. They are reluctant to disclose their income in the same kind of way as they are reluctant to disclose their age. Like sex, you only talk about your personal money matters in carefully selected company. When you ask for a statement it is handed to you discreetly in a plain envelope. To ask to see the manager in his inner sanctum, is like asking to enter the confessional within the Holy of Holies.

2 *Personal service*

The intimate personal service which a bank renders to its customers is, I believe, an immensely valuable contribution to the well-being of men and women, and not least to the well-being of the young. I like particularly the emphasis on this personal ministry (for such it is) in recent bank advertising. For if the possession of a cheque book is a symbol that a young man or young woman is growing up, the bank behind the cheque book is a reminder that sound advice and counsel are often needed for the proper exercise of that responsibility.

This pastoral ministry or (if you like) this ministry of good advice, once the monopoly of the churches, is now (rightly I believe) shared out by a host of professions and welfare agencies in our modern state. The bank has a real part to play in this personal ministry. And to some employees at least, to work in a bank is not just a way of earning a living in a respectable profession. To some, at least, it can seem quite naturally to be the job that God wants them to do for the sake of his people—and a job of real importance.

When, as quite often happens, young men and women give my name as a reference when applying for a job in a bank, I always treat this request with very great seriousness. For I know that banks need, and the work demands, men and women of high calibre and appropriate personality, for here, as much as anywhere, diligence, integrity, honesty, and perseverance are essential qualities.

I know that personal contact over the counter is only a small part of the banker's job. There are the lofty areas of high finance which are as strangely bewildering to me as the intricacies of ecclesiastical politics may be for you.

3 *Finance and the community*

But I know enough to see that the right handling of money is basic to the well-being and stability not only of our own country, but of this whole shrinking world. Finance has a formative role to play in the creation of community. Without the aid of the banks, industrial, commercial, and civic

110

expansion—involving the livelihood of millions—would be an impossibility. And the biblical reminder that we are members one of another has its clear application in the financial world. Currency is one of the ways by which human beings communicate with one another. So it was natural that the television programmes dealing with the recent Budget should not only show interviews with politicians and economists in this country, but almost immediately should also take us over to Zurich to see what the bankers—the famous 'Zurich gnomes'—had to say about the Chancellor's proposals.

In the search for the secret of a true world community, economics has as important a role to play as politics and religion. And within the economic ordering of things, the banks have their huge share of responsibility and influence.

There was a time when the churches tended to give the impression that money was a rather dirty business, even though they had a reputation for always asking for it themselves. Expressions such as 'filthy lucre' were heard from time to time in pulpits. And the Bible is certainly right in saying that money can be the root of all kinds of evil (1 Tim. 6.10). Bank managers must know this every bit as well as parsons, if not better.

4 *Responsible stewardship*

It is coming to be seen more and more clearly that the right use of money is absolutely essential both for personal well-being, and for the health of nations and communities. Money is seen to be one of those apparently physical things which in their right use or misuse convey spiritual realities and basic values. The responsible handling of finance, whether in one's own personal accounts or in the budget of nations and international business or political concerns, cannot therefore any longer be kept in a separate compartment from our thinking about God and his Church and God's purpose for the world.

My use of money—no less than my own use of sex, or of health, or of leisure, or of energy, or of work—is an essential part of my stewardship under God of the talents which I have been given. This is true of me as an individual. It is true as a member of a city, of a nation, of a world. Those who help me, both as a person and as a citizen to exercise that responsibility with integrity and with prudence, are in a true sense ministers under God. That is why the representatives of a great bank, however great or small their own personal part in the work may be, do well to come together from time to time to see the task which they have been given within the perspective of God's purpose for them and for the men and women they serve. It is no mere formality or empty gesture which leads you and your fellow workers in Lloyd's Bank in many parts of the country at this very time, to come into a church and say, 'O God, thank you for the job you have given us to do. Help us to do it as well as we may and as well as you want. For we know that in so far as we are of service to your people for their welfare, we are being of service to you for your greater Glory.'

29   WOMEN AND MEN

at a service for representatives of women's organizations

This address was given at the service which inaugurates each year the conference of the National Council of Women. Its theme, much discussed in church circles today, is the relationship of men and women both in the life of the Church and in secular society. The biblical focus is on the text, 'It is not good for man to be alone' in the second story of Creation (Gen. 2.5–25) *and in St Paul's picture of human relations in Christ when former distinctions (such as male and female) are done away* (Gal. 3.26–29). *Most congregations hear sermons from time to time on the Christian approach to questions of marriage and divorce. Teaching on the wider aspects of men–women relationships and human sexuality is less often heard. This is a subject which is relevant to many aspects of the agenda of the National Council of Women. But there are a number of other occasions when the biblical and theological understanding of sexuality could appropriately be made the theme of an address on a subject of great significance for the well-being of human relations today.*

1 *'Not good to be alone'*
For a text I refer you to that marvellous sentence put into the mouth of God in the second chapter of the book of Genesis

112

when—contemplating the solitary Adam—he says: 'It is not good for man to be alone.' Let me remind you, too, of the context. The sky and the earth have been made, but no life, no vegetation, no animals. Only man sits there on the bare earth, naked and alone. 'This is not good,' says God. Man must have a partner. And he creates the animal kingdom—elephants and fleas, hippopotami and giraffes. The whole circus parade passes before Adam who is fascinated by what he sees and appropriately names each creature as it goes by him. But at the end of the day he remains alone. No partner for him here.

Then in the myth which is as lovely as it is profound, we are told how woman is created for man. He immediately recognizes in her a complementary part of himself, in body and mind made to fit with her, like the other piece of a jig-saw. So that ever afterwards whenever a boy and a girl have fallen in love, as they hold hands under the trees, 'We are made for each other,' they say. And they speak no less than the truth.

But what they perhaps—like so many of us—fail to recognize is that man and woman are made for each other not just for falling in love and for marriage, not just for the creation of children and the making of homes, but for the whole business of living. It is sad that in our misuse of language today such a phrase as 'sexual intercourse' has been narrowed down to mean the physical act of sex. Surely it should have been broadened out to signify the whole creative dialogue between man and woman, a dialogue which should provide insight and power wherever decisions have to be made in the business of our common life together.

2 *Women in society*

This century has rightly stressed the role that women can play in society, and a revolution in the relationship between the sexes is taking place with increasing momentum. Improved standards of living, better health, and family planning are enabling more and more married women to play a major role in the total life of the community, a role which can more than offset the decline of the spinster whose great contribution in the past has been too often taken for granted.

Equal opportunity for education at every level is now rightly leading to an increased demand for equal pay for equal

113

work and responsibility. There are certain professions, notably my own, which continue to set a lamentable example by providing neither equal opportunity nor equal pay, and for reasons which bear very little examination. And there are other places, too, where the battle for equal rights and equal opportunities for both sexes must continue to be fought. But in the end, more important than the rights which one sex has over and against the other, is the actual relationship which ought to exist between the sexes.

What did God create sex for? Is sexuality only to do with that particular relationship called marriage? And is the creative act between man and woman only to be seen in the conception and rearing of children?

3 *Male and female*

Marriage was ordained, says the old Church of England wedding service, for the 'mutual society, help and comfort that the one ought to have of the other'. But why restrict this to marriage? Society, help and comfort—isn't this precisely what men and women can give to one another in every part of life when their relationships are right. Isn't this what sexuality is all about, in the providence of God—the creative meeting of men and women at every level?

It is not therefore equal rights, nor the much-vaunted stereotyped characteristics of maleness and femaleness which should be our main concern, but the interplay of these characteristics in a sexual intercourse which can genuinely create all that is necessary and right for human well-being.

What worries me about the Church to which I belong (and indeed this is true of the greater part of Christendom), is not simply that women are not admitted to the order of priesthood. This is bound to come sooner or later, and then we shall wonder why it was delayed so long. No, what worries me is that, in the meantime, the very places in church life where policy is formulated and decisions are made, are places where, by and large, men sit alone. As a result, the Church often looks like an organization for women run by men. The God-given fact of creative sexuality is allowed precious little opportunity in the very place where you would most expect the gifts of God to be taken with seriousness. Yet the Church is

114

only reflecting public opinion to a great extent, and it is the wider issues which must be our concern here.

At the heart of the Christian gospel—as of the Jewish faith from which it sprang—is a concern for right relationships: right relationships between God and man, and between man and man. St Paul saw in the earliest Christian communities the miracle of the breaking down of barriers. The cultural, political, industrial and racial blocks which divided society in the first century (as they still do today) were seen to dissolve in the presence of Christian love and understanding. Amongst these barriers was that between the sexes. *There is no such thing as Jew and Greek, slave and freeman, male and female; for you are all one person in Christ Jesus.* (Gal. 3.28–29)

Note how, in the Christian dispensation, race does not disappear, nor do the necessary distinctions between bosses and workers, or Greeks and non-Greeks. The distinctions do not disappear, but these differences, instead of being destructive to community as they have been in the past, become creative of it.

The same is true of sex. Maleness and femaleness are not done away in Christ. The Christian is not called to be a-sexual, or religiously neutered. Sexuality is to reach its full creative potential in the establishment of right relationships between men and women in every part of life, not only in marriage but also in politics; not only in the church but also in public life, in industry, in art, and wherever else life is really lived.

4 *Creative partnership*

Indeed this is exactly where we, who dare to call ourselves Christians, ought to be exercising a prophetic ministry to society all around us. For if we, who claim to have the mind of Christ, have not got our relationships right, no wonder the world has got them lopsided too.

Looking at your splendid agenda for this week's conference, with its concern for the welfare of children, the disabled and the elderly; for the place of women under the law and especially in relation to employment; for students as they prepare for their life's work; for safety on the road and in the home; and for the great matters of life and death which the voluntary euthanasia issue raises so acutely, it is clear that men and women need to work together as equal partners with that 'mutual society, help and comfort which each ought to have of the other'. Only in this creative relationship will the answers to these life questions be found; only in this creative relationship, precisely because this is what God intended sex to be all about.

I suppose the time ought to come when single-sex organizations will no longer have a job to do. And indeed Rotarians and Soroptimists, the Mothers' Union and Men's Societies, and (if I may dare say so) your own National Council should already be beginning, at least, to examine very critically (as no doubt you already do) the reasons for their continued one-sex existence.

Certainly we must make it absolutely clear that as Christian people are entrusted with the message of reconciliation, so at the heart of every organization which seeks to co-operate with God in his task of creating the good society, the great quest is for the creation of right relationships. We must break down all the barriers which frustrate those relationships, and within all this (indeed at its very centre), we must discover the right relationship between men and women together in response to their Creator God who, at the very beginning of time, brought Eve to solitary Adam, saying that it was not good for man to be alone.

30 'WHY STAND THERE LOOKING UP INTO THE SKY?'

an Ascension Day sermon in a university chapel

A number of circumstances combined to make the preaching of this sermon a 'special occasion'. Initially it was given in response to an invitation to preach at the Sunday morning service in King's College Chapel in the University of Aberdeen. The date was fixed for the Sunday after Ascension Day. This dictated the biblical theme. Whilst the sermon was in preparation, the Bishop of Durham's comments on the Virgin Birth, the Resurrection, and other miraculous elements

116

in the story of Jesus were exciting much public interest and controversy. It was clearly impossible at that time to speak to a university congregation without reference to the discussion which Bishop Jenkins had stirred up. A third element which had to be taken into consideration was the fact that on this particular Sunday the university was holding its General Council, and there would be a number of former students in the chapel that morning. It was requested that some mention should be made of this by the preacher. All these factors created a 'special occasion' which had to be woven into the address. Obviously some of the material used, which could be dealt with frankly in a university setting, would be inappropriate in a village church. The same gospel would be preached. The way of doing it would be different.

1 The Ascension of Christ

I remember being invited to preach one Ascension Day to a boys' school in Liverpool. 'You don't have to believe,' I told them, 'that Jesus actually stood on a hill and was seen to float up into the sky and vanish. Any more than if I tell you that your headmaster has been set over your school, you'd expect to find him floating about amongst the chimney pots. When you go up in class, you remain physically on the same level as you were before. It's a way,' I told them, 'of talking about authority, about status and power. Going up. Being set over. On top of things.'

As soon as I had finished my sermon, hopefully having persuaded them not to worry their heads too much about the literal details of the Ascension story, the chaplain announced the next hymn. We will now sing, he said:

Hail the Day that sees him rise
To his throne above the skies

And we are back at square one! This just shows how difficult it is for a preacher today to handle much of the stuff of the Bible in the light of contemporary knowledge and thought.

The Roman Catholic theologian Hans Küng, in his recent, much acclaimed book *Eternal Life* comments that there is nothing particularly Christian about an ascent into heaven. It is an idea widespread amongst the religions of the past. We hear, he says, of an Ascension not only in connection with

Enoch and Elijah in the Old Testament, but also with other great figures of antiquity like Hercules, Romulus and Alexander the Great. The Roman historian Suetonius in his biography of Augustus, tells how a Roman officer of praetorian rank swore that he saw the form of the deceased Emperor on its way to heaven after the body had been reduced to ashes.

A casual visitor to this chapel service this morning might well be excused for wondering what on earth the staff and students of a great and famous university were up to, in the year 1984, solemnly reading stories about a Jewish man who is said to have gone up into the sky and vanished 2000 years ago—and why they are singing hymns about it.

It is the stories in the New Testament about the beginning and the end of the life of Jesus of Nazareth which cause us most difficulty these days. And these are the stories which lie behind the rumpus in my own Church, the Church of England, caused by the appointment of David Jenkins, the Professor of Theology and Religious Studies in the University of Leeds, to be the next Bishop of Durham. The Church of England house journal, the *Church Times* says that it has had a greater volume of correspondence about this appointment than any other for many years—and overwhelmingly hostile.

2 *Theological controversy*

The fuss was all about some things which the Bishop designate said on a television programme. The matter under discussion was a perennial one, and one of no little importance on a day when we meet for worship to celebrate the Ascension of Christ. What is the relationship between the Jesus of faith—the Jesus Christ we worship, the Jesus Christ we call Saviour and Redeemer—and the Jesus who is the subject of the four Gospels in particular? What are we to make of the stories of the conception and birth of Jesus on the one hand, and the accounts of the Resurrection and Ascension, the empty tomb, the stone rolled away, the angels, the journey into space—on the other? To believe in the Jesus Christ of faith and devotion, do we really have to accept every alleged particular of the human life of Jesus as told by Matthew, Mark, Luke and John?

The popular press quickly pounced on the answers Professor

118

Jenkins gave to these questions—not because they or their readers normally show a consuming interest in the doctrine of the Incarnation but because they scented ecclesiastical scandal in the air caused by a man about to become a Bishop. In such devious ways serious religious matters come to the attention of the British public. What were the offending words?

On the Virgin Birth, Professor Jenkins said that he was pretty clear that it was a story told after the event, told in order to express and symbolize that Jesus was a unique event from God. 'I wouldn't put it past God,' he said 'to arrange a virgin birth if he wanted to. But I very much doubt if he would.' On the details of the Resurrection accounts he said: 'It does not seem to me that there was any *one* event which you could identify. But it was not a question of people making it up. There was more to it than just Peter's imagination or my imagination. God caused something to happen. It was not just a hallucination, and if you like to call it a miracle—OK.'

Of course on a popular short-hand medium like an off-the-cuff television interview, that kind of thing can quickly be misunderstood. But what Professor Jenkins said in that programme would not surprise anyone in touch with present-day theological thought—either Protestant or Roman Catholic. Indeed Clifford Longley, *The Times* religious affairs correspondent, described him as a fairly conservative modern liberal, not untypical of the Church of England as a whole.

What is of interest and importance here is not what Professor Jenkins said, but the Shock! Horror! reaction of many people, to it, including many ordained ministers of the Church. The Bishop of Durham rumpus illustrates the widening gap between the professional Bible scholars and theologians, and many ordinary clergy in their pulpits and the people in the pews. For too long we ministers have tended to underestimate the intelligence of the laity we preach to, Sunday by Sunday, keeping the insights of Bible Scholarship and theology away from our congregations in a 'not in front of the children attitude'.

We desperately need to have a much more critical and a much more open discussion of our exploration into God in our churches—and much more honesty, too, on all sides. And if some people who have been over-protected by a narrow, nerve-wracked biblical literalism, may be shocked by what they hear, far more people (and not only the young) will be liberated and helped forward in the Christian experience.

All this is very relevant to the theme of this Sunday—the Ascension. What is it all about? First, we always have to remember that the earliest New Testament writings, the first Epistles of St Paul, came before the Gospels were written and show remarkably little interest in the earthly life of Jesus. The central focus was on the overwhelming experience of those early Christians of the saving power of the living Lord, and of his claim upon their lives.

3 A conquering faith

I live—but not I—it is Christ who lives in me. (Gal. 2.20)

Of course in due time eye-witnesses, and those who heard at first or second or third hand from eye-witnesses began to write down what could be remembered of the life and death and resurrection of Jesus, because it was from such facts that the powerful new faith had sprung. But the gospel compilers were not reporters in the modern sense of the word, so it is not easy for us at this distance to disentangle factual record, legend, pious imagination and theological comment. Exactly what happened on the first Easter morning which we have recently been celebrating, or at that problematic event, the Ascension, on which we have focused today, we can never know for sure. What matters to us is that in these gospel records, in the whole range of material from historical fact to theological myth, lies the strong conviction and witness of those first Christians who knew that in Jesus—risen, ascended and alive—they were seeing an image of God and experiencing the power of God for real.

That conviction and experience can still be ours two thousand years later: the certainty of the victory of love over hate, of truth over lies, of life over death; the faith in which we are more than conquerors through Christ our Lord.

You may wonder why Luke, who was not an eye-witness and who wrote about these things perhaps forty years after they happened, should crown his story of the early life of Jesus with a dramatic picture of his ascent into heaven like a king on

120

his coronation day mounting to his appointed throne. Isn't the answer that Jesus of Nazareth was now known to be the reigning, conquering King, set to rule over that kingdom of compassion, humility, peace, justice and forgiveness which was at the core of his message in word and in deed. This kingdom remains for all time the ultimate touchstone for the well-being of mankind, and this is why he taught us to pray: 'Your kingdom come *on earth*'.

On earth because Christianity is not about 'pie in the sky when you die'. Leave that till the time comes. What matters at this moment is the coming of God's kingdom here and now.

There's a wonderful twist in Luke's story of the Ascension. Jesus vanishes into the cloud. The disciples stand open-mouthed, wide-eyed, gazing into space, waiting for the come-back. And an impatient voice from heaven calls out to them: *Why do you stand there looking up into the sky when there's a job to be done here on earth?* (Acts 1.11) A condemnation, if ever there was one, of all who use Christ's religion as an escape from the here-and-now into some religious cloud-cuckoo land!

4 *Christ the King*

'Rejoice the Lord is King' we sang at the beginning of this service. In a few minutes we shall be singing 'Crown him with many crowns'. But a king is no good without a kingdom. And a kingdom doesn't happen without responsive and responsible subjects. No good gazing up into the sky when there is God's work to be done here.

Take a look at our political rivalry, our industrial confrontations, our broken marriages and broken-up homes, our unequal opportunities for education and work, our deep-down prejudice of race, sex, class and nationality, our sterile economic system, our corporate greed, our unequal division of the earth's good things between the rich minority and the poor majority. You only have to look—to question. *Rejoice the Lord is King?* Dare we sing it when all the evidence is that he is not yet King—because we won't let him be.

Have you ever tried seriously in your own mind to work out the practical implications of Jesus Christ's teaching about the Kingdom for our tragic world? It's an exercise worth doing. It's also worth trying to work it out—if you dare—for your

121

own personal life-style too: not just your religion, but your work, your finances, your family, your friendships, your priorities.

We are in King's Chapel. The king in question, I suppose, is James IV, though he is dead and buried long ago. But of course this chapel is built in honour of another king—an Ascended King. So it might be worth asking, on this General Council Sunday, whether the thousands over the centuries who have worshipped within these beautiful walls have memories of King's Chapel which are simply nostalgic for the beauty and dignity of it all. Do all those who graduated from here to become doctors and lawyers, politicians, journalists, industrialists, business people, teachers, ministers, farmers, engineers, scholars, community workers and much else besides, remember it as a place to gaze up into the sky—or did they find here an incentive to follow a faith for all the days upon earth, and in all they have to do? Did they learn here that there is a King to be obeyed, and a kingdom to be built? And will this chapel continue to stand as a sure witness to the Kingship of Christ over every discipline and every facet of life for as long as there is a university here in Aberdeen?

Other Mowbray Sermon Outlines
Series Editor: D. W. Cleverley Ford